Decisive Battles of the
PACIFIC
WAR

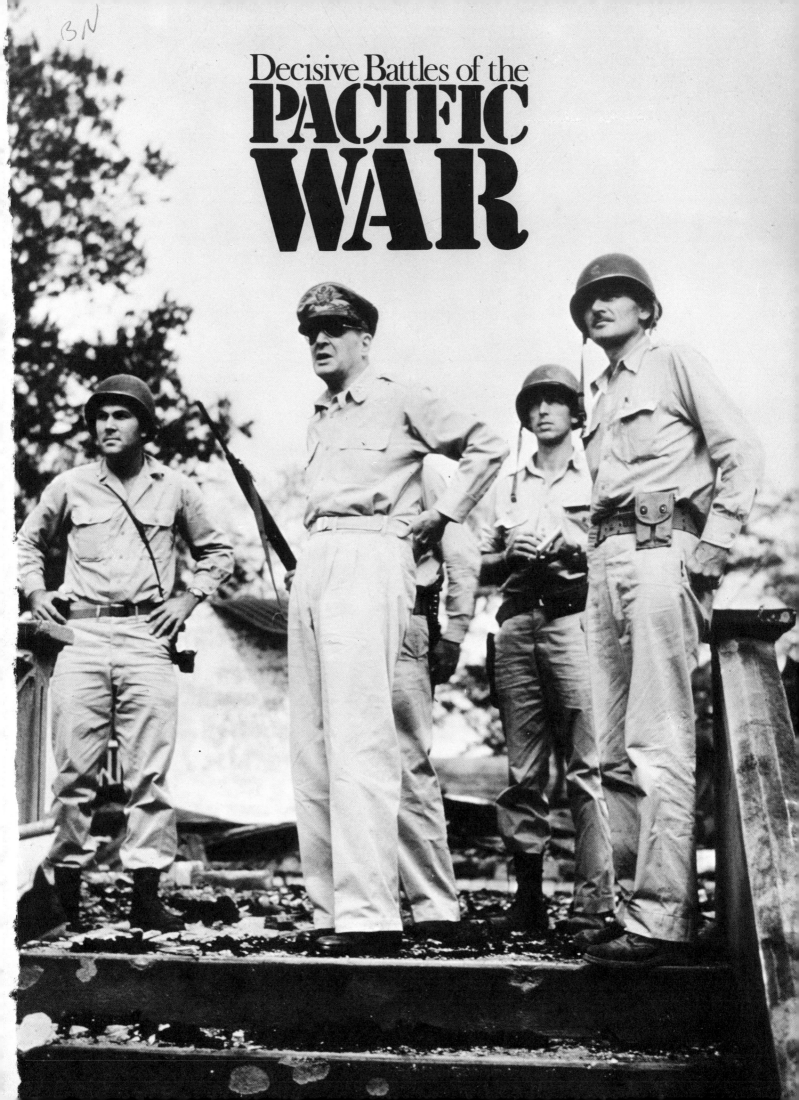

Decisive Battles of the
PACIFIC WAR

EDITED BY ANTONY PRESTON

CHARTWELL BOOKS INC.
Published by Chartwell Books Inc.
A Division of Book Sales Inc.
110 Enterprise Avenue
Secaucus, New Jersey 07094

A BISON BOOK

First published in the United States of America by
Chartwell Books Inc.
A Division of Book Sales Inc.
110 Enterprise Avenue
Secaucus, New Jersey, 07094

Copyright © 1979 by Bison Books Limited

Produced by
Bison Books Limited
4 Cromwell Place
London SW 7

ISBN: 0 89009 293 1

Library of Congress Catalog Card Number: 79 53075

Printed in Hong Kong

CONTENTS

Roosevelt and Churchill meet to discuss peace aims aboard the HMS *Prince of Wales* on 10 August 1941. This conference took place off Newfoundland and resulted in the issuing of the Atlantic Charter. The meeting had been called to discuss Allied aims and even though the USA was not at war, Roosevelt pledged more aid to Great Britain and agreed on the 'Germany First' principle, which meant that the commanders in the Pacific War had to fight to get their share of resources. On Roosevelt's right, leaning forward, is General George Marshall, Army Chief of Staff, and on his left stands Admiral Ernest King, Commander in Chief of Naval Forces. King believed that naval and army forces in the Pacific deserved a greater share of resources and he was constantly putting forward his view in Joint Chief of Staff meetings.

INTRODUCTION
By Antony Preston

The war which broke out between the United States and its allies and the Japanese Empire was a truly titanic struggle. In its course two colonial dominions were destroyed, and a mighty and seemingly invincible modern military power was destroyed. The campaigns were waged on a massive scale, across the wastes of the Pacific, and they were finally decided by the dropping of the atom bomb, a decision which altered the destiny of the whole world. Small wonder that the battles of the Pacific still fascinate students of geopolitical and military history.

The first battle, the attack on Pearl Harbor is deceptively simple: surprise attack on an unprepared base, with catastrophic losses to the defenders and negligible losses to the attackers. The implications, however, were profound and far-reaching. Strategically Pearl Harbor made the Second European Civil War into a World War by arousing American public opinion to the extent that isolationism was swept away in an instant. Tactically Pearl Harbor achieved what the Japanese planners had hoped: the immobilization of the American Pacific Fleet and destruction of the bombers on Oahu. But

it failed to catch the three aircraft carriers, a failure which was to lead to a severe Japanese defeat six months later. On a lesser scale, by failing to destroy the oil reserves the Japanese left the base in working order, ready to support a new fleet. For the US Navy Pearl Harbor was a blessing in disguise. By knocking out the battleships the Japanese forced the admirals to go straight to the concept of the fast carrier task force, rather than the intermediate stage of tying the carriers down to operating with slow battleships.

With the benefit of hindsight it is easy to ask how the Japanese could be so misguided as to antagonize the United States for such a catchpenny victory, and to take on the industrial might of the West with so little thought for the consequences. The answer is complex and has much to do with the previous century of Japanese history.

Japan had created a modern industrial society in about half the time taken by a comparable European state. After the restoration of the Meiji Dynasty progress was unbelievably rapid, and as Japan's industrial power grew her Army and Navy were able to improve their

efficiency with new weapons and training methods. By 1896 the Navy was formidable, and dispatched the inefficient Chinese forces at the Battle of the Yalu River. A much more testing campaign was launched in 1904 to dislodge Russia from her foothold in Manchuria, but to the astonishment of the world, the Japanese Army took the fortress of Port Arthur and defeated the Russian Army with apparent ease. Even more miraculous was the destruction of the Russian Fleet at the Battle of Tsushima, the first naval battle of modern times. The Japanese sank or captured almost the entire fleet of Admiral Rozhestvensky and showed that their training and materiel were sufficient to humble the third-ranking European navy.

Was it surprising that the Japanese military began to think that they were as good as the best in the world? Their admirers, who had no reason to like the Russians, fostered this view. The First World War accelerated the growth of Japanese industry as huge orders for munitions and ships poured in from the British and French; by November 1918 over 250 merchant ships had been built for the Allies and the Japanese mercantile marine itself had reached a level of two million tons.

Being a newly industrialized nation Japan felt the effects of the post-war slump very soon. The rise in per capita income had also brought in its train a rise in population, and to maintain expectations for these teeming millions Japan needed markets and access to raw materials. But these were in the hands of Western countries, principally Great Britain, the Netherlands and the USA, and they too wished to preserve their position. Unable to dominate markets and deprived of access to such vital raw materials as rubber, tin and oil, Japan found herself looking at other ways of ensuring her economic survival. Given the historical precedent of the *samurai* warrior-caste and its role in administration, coupled with the heroic achievements of the armed forces against Russia in 1904-05, it is hardly surprising that a military solution was chosen. The Army was the most powerful voice in government, answerable to the Emperor alone and run by an ambitious and arrogant officer-caste, but the Navy was also keen to prove itself against all-comers.

The destroyer *Shaw* was in drydock at Pearl Harbor when the Japanese torpedo and dive bombers attacked. The explosion of her forward 5-inch magazines provided a spectacular pyrotechnic display. The damage sustained by the US Far East Fleet was not irreparable and all three fleet carriers escaped because they were out on missions.

An early picture of Roosevelt and his Cabinet in May 1934. On board the USS *Indianapolis* they were reviewing the Fleet.

To the outside world Japan was a monolithic country, a hard-working, militaristic nation run with ruthless efficiency and dedication. But in reality it was riven by factions inside and outside the armed forces. These rivalries, coupled with the harsh economic realities, made military adventures almost unavoidable. The ease with which China was invaded proved illusory, and after a hard-fought campaign the resources of Malaya and the East Indies were still out of reach. The Army was stretched to its limits in trying to subdue China, and so the Navy was called in to provide a strategic plan which would achieve the grand design. This was the genesis of the Pearl Harbor plan, not so much a bold first stroke as a gambler's throw.

In the weeks after Pearl Harbor the Japanese advanced rapidly across the Pacific, expelling the British and Dutch from their possessions with ridiculous ease. The defensive perimeter islands demanded by the Navy as its security for a campaign against the US Navy were all seized as planned, within the deadline demanded the Commander in Chief, Admiral Yamamoto. But he still hankered after a decisive battle to eliminate the aircraft carriers which had escaped the debacle at Pearl Harbor. The Army was also keen to keep up its momentum, and so the fatal decision to occupy the Solomons was taken in April 1942.

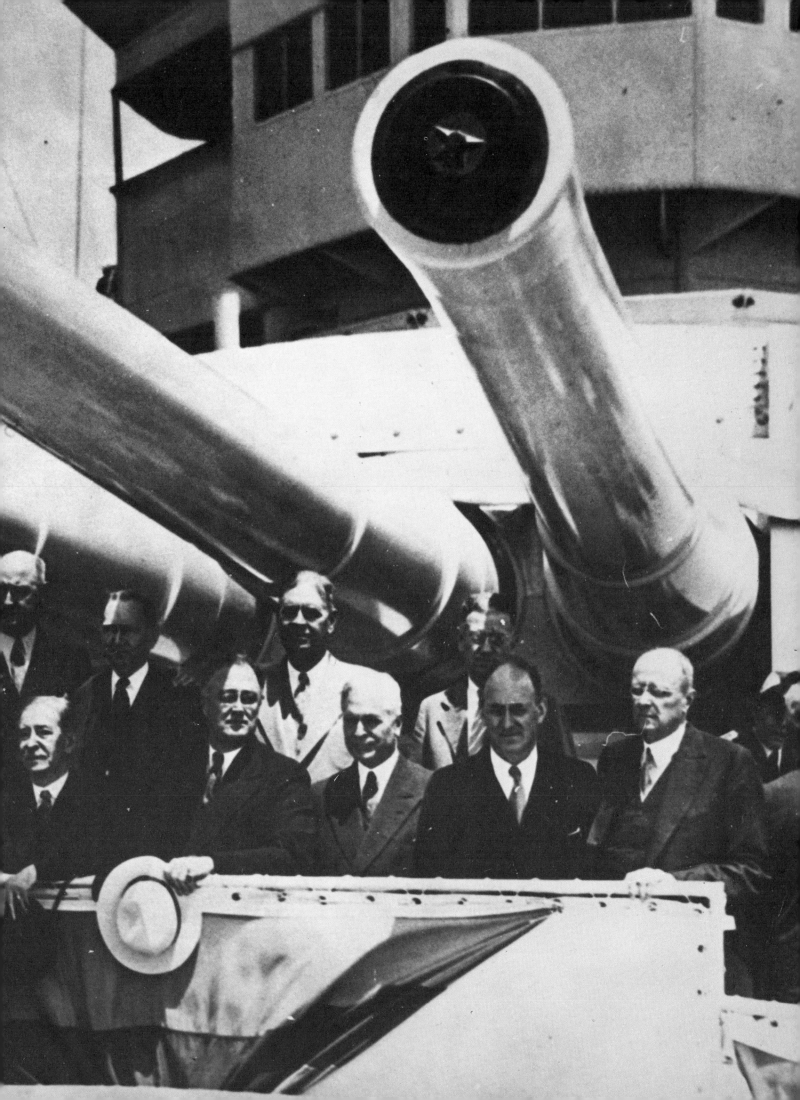

Rear Admiral Osami Nagano, Chief of Japanese Naval Staff during World War II. He was responsible for overall strategy.

Rear Admiral Shigetaro Shimada, Imperial Japanese Navy Minister during World War II.

The Battle of the Coral Sea which resulted was indecisive because it was the first carrier-vs-carrier battle ever fought, and neither side knew how best to use their carriers. In military terms it was a minor tactical defeat for the Americans, but for the Japanese it was a strategic defeat. They had failed to cut communications between Pearl Harbor and Australia, and so could not prevent the build-up of strength in the Southwest Pacific. The consequences were not immediately perceived by the Japanese, but when they tried to consolidate their position in the Solomons three months later the American reaction was much faster and more positive because of their secure base in Australia.

The Battle of Midway was the outcome of a much more ambitious plan to trap the American carriers. This time the disparity between the two sides was big enough to make a Japanese victory almost certain. But numbers cannot prevail against an enemy who has superior intelligence and the opportunity to choose when and where he wants to fight. Midway was not as decisive as the US Navy thought, for despite the loss of six fast carriers and 55 percent of their pilots there were enough new carriers to rebuild carrier task groups. What was achieved at Midway was psychological as much as material. For the first time the Japanese realized that their opponents were not grossly inferior in courage and determination. They also realized that they had been outwitted at every turn by the Americans, and still the dangerous carriers had not been eliminated. For the Allies Midway was a tremendous fillip. Having treated the Japanese with contempt for too long, the British and Americans had, since December 1941, regarded them as supermen, but now they had been massively defeated in a fight between the whole Combined Fleet and three carriers.

Midway also marked the high-water mark of Japanese expansion. Thereafter the Americans took the initiative and never lost it. It was not, to quote Churchill, the beginning of the end, but it was the end of the beginning.

The long struggle for Guadalcanal was a prime example of the Japanese inability to decide when to stop expansion. The first move in the drive on Australia had been a move to the Solomons and an overland attack on Port Moresby in New Guinea. After Midway the

Army suggested that the time had come to consolidate and to shorten lines of communication, but the Navy refused to abandon any of its gains in the Southwest Pacific. Although doomed to fight a defensive war until such time as it could recreate the superb aircrews which had done so well six months before, it was prepared to defend a series of individually worthless islands. This in turn meant a drain on those same aircrew, with the result that the carrier air groups never regained the proficiency that had made them so dangerous.

The battle for Guadalcanal, a series of bloody engagements on land and sea, may have cost the United States and its allies a great deal but the cost to the Japanese was much greater. Despite all the ingenuity and bravery that they could muster the Japanese were eventually forced to concede defeat after suffering 25,000 casualties. The spirit of the *samurai* produced wonderful heroism and devotion to duty, but it also induced a lopsided view of strategic priorities, and from Guadalcanal onwards the strategic judgment of the Japanese became noticeably worse. Tactically Guadalcanal showed the Japanese at their best, however, for their ships dominated the waters around the Solomons in a series of fierce night actions fought around reinforcements of ground troops. The combination of the deadly Long Lance torpedo and superb night-fighting techniques put the Allied ships on the defensive, and only radar could tip the scales the other way.

Guadalcanal was only a holding operation for the Allies, but once the Solomons were secure the way was open for a series of mighty blows against the island perimeter and the liberation of the Philippines. But before the Philippines could be attacked the fortress islands of Saipan, Tinian and Guam, in the Marianas group, had to be neutralized. Almost incidentally the assault on the Marianas also brought about the destruction of Japanese naval air power, and although the Americans were to debate the battle subsequently with considerable bitterness the 'Marianas Turkey Shoot' paved the way for the final victory. Politically the fall of Saipan in June-July 1944 marks the first serious blow to military prestige in Japan's ruling hierarchy; the government of General Tojo fell, and faith in the military was weakened.

The true benefits of the Philippine Sea battle were not appreciated even at Leyte, for it was not known until afterward that the carriers in that battle had no aircraft because there were no pilots to fly them. For the Americans the liberation of the Philippines was a matter of keeping faith and redeeming a promise made by General MacArthur, rather than a direct military necessity, and knowing that the Japanese made their despairing final attempt to destroy the American fleet. Three major battles made up the total Leyte battle, the largest naval action in history, with battleships engaging one another, destroyers facing capital ships with torpedoes and carriers launching attacks against surface ships at sea. The critics of Admiral Spruance had attacked his caution at the end of the Battle of the Philippine Sea, but his strongest critic, Admiral Halsey, gave a frighteningly vivid example of what could go wrong through recklessness. The desperate rearguard action off Samar was a brutal reminder that navies exist to protect communications and shipping, not specifically to sink enemy warships.

Nobody in World War II seriously questioned the validity of strategic bombing and so it is futile to criticize the American commitment to bomb Japan into surrender. In any case the islands taken to provide airfields for B-29 bombers, Saipan and Okinawa in particular, would have had to be captured or neutralized before a seaborne assault could be attempted against the home islands. Also, part of the purpose of strategic bombing is to give one's own side a feeling of 'hitting back,' and as early as 1942 the Doolittle Raid from the USS *Hornet* had played a small part in restoring American morale after a chain of unbroken gloom and disaster.

The critics of the atom bomb conveniently forget the horrific casualties caused by 'clean' incendiary bombs and high explosive on Japanese cities. The major cities became almost uninhabitable once the B-29s began missions from the Marianas, and the weight of bombing rose even further once Okinawa was in use after April 1945. Thus the carnage of Hiroshima and Nagasaki was cruelly irrelevant; even those two blows had no effect on the question of surrender. When surrender finally came it was because of the intervention of the Emperor on the side of a peace faction, rather

The scene on the beach at Okinawa shortly after the US had landed. Okinawa was the last hurdle for the US to conquer in preparation for the invasion of Japan.

than a widespread reluctance to continue the war.

The requirements of the bombing campaign led to the costly assault on Iwo Jima, for there could be no other military reason for sacrificing 25,000 Americans to capture this obscure island. But it was equally reckless for the Japanese to expend so much blood to defend it, and Iwo Jima must be one of World War II's grimmest monuments to human stubbornness.

The horrors of Iwo Jima were repeated on Okinawa, but with a significant difference. For the first time the bombarding ships standing off shore were pounded by kamikaze attacks.

In essence the danger of the kamikaze lay in the fact that it was a simple guided missile, with the human brain providing terminal guidance. Its effectiveness led directly to the US Navy's 'Bumblebee' program to perfect an anti-aircraft guided weapon, although the results were not to come to fruition for another ten years. Okinawa came as a great shock to the US Navy, for during the previous three years the tactics of protecting the carriers by AA gunfire, while allowing the carrier's aircraft to provide the prime defense against air attack, had been good enough. The kamikazes showed that existing anti-aircraft guns were all but useless against this form of attack.

The fall of Okinawa was the end of the greatest war the world has ever seen. The major battles of that war are described in the pages that follow, and before digesting the detailed descriptions it is well to ponder the question of whether it could all have been avoided. My own feeling is that it could not, for the reasons already given. We are all prisoners of our history, and the Japanese had evolved a way of life and a philosophy which dictated a military solution to their problems. As for the atom bomb, while it is hard to pretend that the seaborne blockade could not have eventually starved Japan into surrender of some sort, military occupation would have been needed to end the war. And, given the bloodshed and suffering of the previous four years, can one seriously maintain that President Truman would have been justified in gambling the estimated one million casualties to be suffered in an invasion of Japan against the distinct possibility of shocking Japan into immediate surrender? More to the point, would anyone have *allowed* him to make the choice?

ANTONY PRESTON
London, February 1979

An aerial view of Pearl
Harbor a few months before
the Day of Infamy.

1 PEARL HARBOR
The Day of Infamy

Brigadier General William (Billy) Mitchell was an air theorist of some importance during the interwar period. After service in France in the latter part of World War I as Aviation Officer in the American Expeditionary Force, he was convinced that the future of modern warfare lay inextricably with the airplane, particularly in its strategic role. He was an admirer of Lord Trenchard, the British Commander of the Royal Flying Corps on the Western Front who had become Chief of the Air Staff when the RAF was formed in 1918, and envious of the independence gained by the British air arm. In an attempt to achieve a similar state for the American air services, split as they were between the Army, Navy and the Marine Corps, he put forward the argument that, so far as the United States was concerned, air power was the most important form of defense applicable to the future. Armies were expensive and took time to ship out to trouble spots; navies were inflexible and extremely vulnerable to air attack. His attempt to prove the latter point was dramatic and, as it turned out, alarmingly prophetic.

In 1921 Mitchell received permission to try out a series of experiments involving the bombing of capital ships. After trials with dummy

bombs, which proved nothing, he was allowed to go one stage further, using the supposedly unsinkable German battleship *Ostfriesland*, surrendered to the Allies in 1919 and by now little more than a hulk. Stationing the vessel some 60 miles off the Virginia coast, a squadron of Martin bombers, armed with specially designed 2000lb bombs, attacked on 21 July 1921. Within a matter of minutes, the ship had turned turtle and sunk. Detractors immediately pointed out that the experiment would have had a different outcome against a fully-armed and protected battleship, able to take evasive action, and the event was conveniently dis-missed as a publicity stunt for Mitchell's campaign of revolutionary thinking. As Mitchell himself was to be court-martialed four years later for an ill-judged attack upon the 'incompetence' of the War Department over the loss of the dirigible *Shenandoah*, it was easy to regard him as something of a crank. But this ignored the most important aspect of the *Ostfriesland* sinking. A new era of naval warfare had arrived, and although it undoubtedly needed technological improvement, the advent of the naval aircraft, capable of attacking capital ships from above, spelled the end of the huge, expensive and vulnerable battleship as the cen-

General 'Billy' Mitchell surrounded by his staff in 1919. Mitchell advocated a separate 'air department' in the 1920s. He also claimed that battleships would become obsolete with the advance of air power. He overstated his case, made enemies and in 1925 was court-martialed and dismissed.

Above: Admiral Husband
Kimmel (center) confers with
Captain Delany (left) and
Captain Smith, his Chief of
Staff in 1941. Kimmel was
Commander in Chief of the
US Pacific Fleet at Pearl
Harbor. Kimmel was held
responsible for the fiasco and
censured. He was removed
from his command on 17
December 1941 and took no
further part in the war.

Right: Admiral Thomas
Hart, Commander of the
US Asiatic Fleet at the time
of the Pearl Harbor attack.
His naval forces were
stationed off the Philippines
and consisted of a few
destroyers, submarines and
motor torpedo boats.

tral feature of fleet organization. Mitchell provided the lesson, but it was not to be appreciated for another 20 years, when the Japanese, using their naval air power based upon aircraft carriers, dealt a stunning blow to American prestige at Pearl Harbor.

War between the United States and Japan seemed inevitable for much of the 1930s. Ever since Japan, intent upon territorial expansion to ease domestic pressures caused by rapid industrialization and a population explosion, had moved into Manchuria in 1932. Encroachments upon the American spheres of influence in China and the Pacific had threatened to escalate into open hostility. But for much of the decade the traditional isolationism of the United States had forced her political leaders to take a conciliatory stance. Even in 1937, when Japan attacked China on a broad front and abrogated a Naval Limitation Treaty signed with America and Britain in 1921 – a treaty which had allowed the Japanese to build only three capital ships for every ten constructed in the West – protests had been the full extent of American reaction. However, by early 1940, with Japanese forces established along the entire Chinese coast and Chiang Kai-shek's Nationalist armies driven inland, the Americans felt obliged to act. Consequently, on 26 January President Roosevelt canceled a Treaty of Commerce with Japan and tried to impose economic sanctions. This had little effect, and as the Japanese became progressively more aggressive, allying themselves defensively to Germany and Italy in September 1940, concluding a non-aggression pact with Russia in April 1941, and actually moving into French Indo-China (now Vietnam), three months later, Roosevelt went one stage further. In July 1941 he 'froze' all Japanese assets in the United States, an act which effectively dried up, for want of cash, all supplies of oil to Japan and forced the Tokyo government to react. Oil was a key commodity, entirely absent from Japanese national or occupied territories. To replace American supplies Japan would either have to give in and accede to Washington's demands for a full withdrawal of forces from China and Indo-China, or attack southward to the oil-rich Dutch East Indies. With a militarist party in power in Tokyo, the choice was obvious: an attack was the only honorable way out.

Plans for such an assault, with the establishment of an economically self-sufficient 'Great East Asia Co-Prosperity Sphere,' had been laid down long before 1941. They owed their origin to a National Defense Policy, formulated as early as 1909. This, for the purposes of fleet maneuvers, had stipulated the United States as a purely hypothetical enemy, but had increased in relevance as the century progressed. It centered upon the assumption that the Americans would take the offensive in the Western Pacific – that is, virtually in Japanese home waters – as soon as hostilities began, and planned the destruction of the US fleet somewhere between the Marianas and Marshall Islands. In other words, the Americans would sail straight into a carefully-laid trap. But things had changed since 1909, particularly so far as Japanese aspirations were concerned, and by the late 1930s revisions were desperately needed. They were provided by Admiral Isoroku Yamamoto.

Appointed Commander in Chief of the Japanese Combined Fleet on 30 August 1939, Yamamoto recognized immediately that existing war plans were unsatisfactory. They were based upon a defensive stance, waiting for the Americans to appear, whereas if hostilities began the exact opposite was intended, with a southward thrust to gain the Dutch East Indies and their essential oil fields before the British, Dutch and Americans could react. This necessitated a concentration of Japanese naval and military power away from the area of intended fleet action, leaving the route to Japan itself dangerously exposed, particularly as the Americans, in May 1940, had moved their Pacific fleet from the West Coast to Pearl Harbor in the Central Pacific island of Oahu, a part of the Hawaiian chain. A westward thrust by this fleet could be decisive, threatening Japan and cutting the vulnerable lines of communication with forces attacking the Dutch East Indies. This led Yamamoto to the conclusion that if war was inevitable, the first Japanese action should be an attack upon Pearl Harbor to destroy the US Pacific fleet at its base. He began to work for this from the start of his command.

At first he had to tread carefully in the face of entrenched opposition from the Naval General Staff, gradually pushing the area of intended fleet action eastward until it included the waters around Hawaii. This was accepted in principle, but as the main part of the Japanese fleet was already earmarked for the protection of the southward push, it seemed a hollow victory. It was then that Yamamoto introduced his trump card – the use of naval aircraft, taking off from a carrier force stationed near Hawaii, to bomb the Americans in a surprise attack. The idea was revolutionary and immediately opposed, but Yamamoto was convinced of its viability. He had always been interested in the capabilities of air power, recognizing it as a crucial new element of naval strategy as early as 1927, and when he was appointed to the aircraft carrier *Akagi* in 1928 he had devoted himself 'to the practical problems involved in the developing theories of air warfare.' By 1937 he was sure in his own mind that attacks by torpedo-carrying aircraft could destroy any battleship then afloat, and that the key to naval supremacy in the future lay with the aircraft carrier and its long-range strike potential. If a force of carriers could approach Hawaii in secret, the war could commence with a powerful aerial strike upon the US fleet in Pearl Harbor, destroying battleships and shore installations to a crippling extent.

Preparations for such an assault began in late 1939, well before the Naval General Staff had given its blessing, with Yamamoto insisting upon a high standard of proficiency in carrier-based attacks throughout the naval air arm. In addition he managed to persuade his superiors to increase the carrier-building program and to authorize the introduction of new naval aircraft. By the end of 1940 Japan was well stocked in both respects. Four carriers – the *Akagi, Kaga, Hiryu* and *Soryu* – were immediately available, with two others – the *Shokaku* and *Zuikaku* – expected to be ready by August 1941; long-range flying boats, capable of carrying 2000lb bomb loads over 800 miles had been introduced into service, and a new fighter aircraft, the A6M Zero, had been put into production. A reliable torpedo bomber, the Nakajima B5N2 (later code named Kate by the Allies), already existed, while the Aichi D3A1 (Val) dive bomber, although approaching obsolescence, was still an adequate machine, capable of inflicting the necessary degree of damage. Taken together, equipment was clearly no problem, but Yamamoto had to gain permission to mount his *coup de main*.

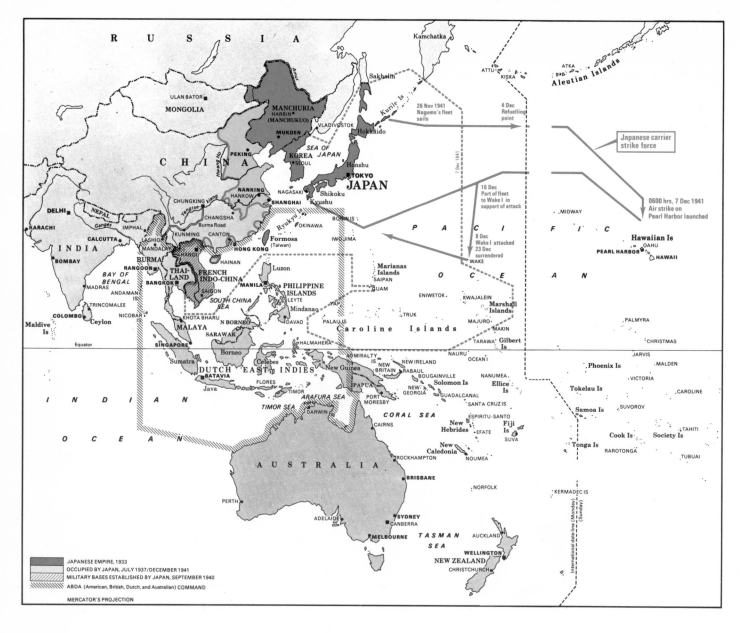

JAPANESE EMPIRE, 1933
OCCUPIED BY JAPAN, JULY 1937/DECEMBER 1941
MILITARY BASES ESTABLISHED BY JAPAN, SEPTEMBER 1940
ABDA (American, British, Dutch, and Australian) COMMAND

MERCATOR'S PROJECTION

Approaching the problem cautiously, he began by building up support from among his own staff, confiding firstly in his Chief of Staff Admiral Shigeru Fukudome and then in Rear Admiral Takajiro Onishi, Chief of Staff of the land-based 11th Air Fleet. It was the latter who introduced Yamamoto to Commander Minoru Genda, a brilliant and experienced naval airman, and it was at this point that the plan started to assume its final form. After ten days of careful study, Genda came to the conclusion that the projected operation was 'difficult but not impossible,' provided that certain changes were made. To begin with, he did not agree with Yamamoto that the main target should be the American battleships, preferring to aim for the destruction of carriers,

particularly as three such vessels – the *Enterprise*, *Lexington* and *Saratoga* – were known to be with the Pacific Fleet. Similarly, he favored far more concentration of force than Yamamoto had envisaged, with all six Japanese carriers taking part, their aircraft making more than one attack if circumstances allowed. Onishi passed these comments on to the Commander in Chief, and Genda was requested to draw up a detailed plan.

This began to take shape toward the end of March 1941 under the code name Operation Z, with Genda gradually expanding the scope of the attack. According to his ideas, a special task force of twenty I-class submarines and five two-man midget submarines would approach Hawaii before war was declared, the former

Japanese Mitsubishi A6Ms, nicknamed Zeros, prepare for take off prior to the Pearl Harbor attack.

Mitsubishi A5M Claude. This aircraft served in the Pacific Theater for about six months after Pearl Harbor until it was phased out.

A Nakajima B5N Kate torpedo bomber takes off from a carrier on 7 December 1941, as the crew cheers 'Banzai.'

stationing themselves around Oahu to catch any American ships that tried to escape, with the latter actually entering Pearl Harbor to add to the chaos caused by the aerial strike. Meanwhile the main force of six carriers, protected by destroyers and cruisers, would take a circuitous route, well away from known shipping lanes, and approach Hawaii from the north, where least expected. A total of 360 aircraft, comprising torpedo bombers, high-level bombers and fighters, would be launched about 230 miles from Oahu, to arrive over Pearl Harbor just after dawn, preferably on a Sunday when the American fleet, following peace-time training routines, would be in harbor with only skeleton crews on board. Once over the anchorage, if surprise was complete the torpedo bombers would attack first, followed closely by the high-level bombers and then the dive bombers, with the fighters providing a protective air umbrella. If surprise had been lost, the fighters would go in first to gain control of the air over the targets, clearing the way for the bombers. Either way, the assaults, to be delivered by two waves of aircraft, would be expected to last no more than two hours all told.

Yamamoto accepted this scheme without reservation, organizing training schedules and making sure that technical problems were solved on time. After sailing round the coast of Japan to find a suitable training area, he chose Kagoshima Bay, south of Kyushu, a spot which bore a striking resemblance to Pearl Harbor, and it was here that his naval pilots, as yet unaware of their projected task, practiced the necessary skills. They quickly attained a very high standard, with dive bombers reducing their release-point to 1500 feet and high-level bombers achieving 80 percent accuracy against stationary targets. At the same time existing torpedoes were modified to take account of the shallow nature of Pearl Harbor (it was only 40 feet deep) and special bombs, capable of cutting through the armor plate of battleships, were introduced. By late October 1941, each pilot, in a series of special briefings on board the *Akagi*, had been assigned to individual targets; Commander Mitsuo Fuchida, an experienced air leader, had been chosen to command the air attack on the day; and the entire force had been placed under Rear Admiral Chuichi Nagumo. All that was missing was permission to go ahead.

This came eventually on 3 November, when Yamamoto and his entire staff threatened to resign unless a decision was made. Even then, there was a continuing possibility of a last-minute cancellation, for the Japanese Emperor was determined to continue diplomatic negotiations with the Americans for as long as possible, in the hope that some kind of compromise could be worked out to prevent his militaristic government going to war. The chances of this occurring seemed fairly remote, however, and Yamamoto took the opportunity to draft his final orders. On 6 November a full-scale dress rehearsal of the attack took place, involving all six carriers, and 350 aircraft staged a successful mock attack on a target 200 miles from the launching zone. Twenty-four hours later Nagumo was informed that Y-day – the day of attack – would be Sunday, 7 December (Hawaii time) and ordered to assemble his fleet at Tankan Bay on Etorofu, the largest of the Kurile Islands, by 22 November. The ships began to leave their bases on 17 November; 27 submarines, known as the Advanced Expeditionary Force, set out for Hawaii between 18 and 20 November. By 22 November all six carriers, together with two battleships,

Above: A torpedo hits the USS *West Virginia* at Pearl Harbor. In the lower left corner of this picture are the USS *Curtiss, Detroit, Raleigh, Utah* and the *Tangier* along the near side of Ford Island: 0800 hours on 7 December 1941.

Left: An Aichi D3A Val dives into action during the height of the Pearl Harbor attack.

Left: Battleship Row seen from a Japanese aircraft. The ships are, left to right, *Nevada, Arizona* and *Vestal, Tennessee* and *West Virginia, Maryland* and *Oklahoma*.

25

Main picture: The USS *Arizona* blows up after she has been hit during the first wave attack on Pearl Harbor.

Inset top: An aerial view of Ford Island and Battleship Row under attack.

Inset bottom: The USS *Shaw*'s magazine blows up.

two heavy cruisers, one light cruiser, nine destroyers and eight fleet tankers, were ready to go. They set sail before dawn on 26 November, following a northerly route in overcast and stormy conditions, hoping to avoid American detection for the whole of their 12-day voyage.

In retrospect, the maintenance of secrecy is surprising, for since August 1940 the Americans had been able to read all Japanese diplomatic communications, having cracked the relevant code. But there was never any direct mention of Operation Z, and so long as negotiations continued in Washington, the possibility of a sudden Japanese attack seemed remote. Even if this had not been the case, there was no reason to suppose that Pearl Harbor would be primary target. It was a long way from Japan, necessitating the formation of a naval force which did not appear to exist (US Intelligence, fooled by false radio traffic, reported all Japanese carriers to be 'still in home waters' as late as 27 November), and seemed contrary to

known Japanese aspirations toward the Dutch East Indies. An aura of complacency gradually emerged, to be reflected tragically in a total lack of defensive preparations in Hawaii. By the weekend of 6/7 December the fleet was still following peacetime routines, aerial reconnaissance was restricted to sea areas to the south and west, torpedo nets across the mouth of the harbor were rarely kept in place, and security was lax. Even when one of the Japanese midget submarines was spotted and sunk by the minesweeper USS *Condor* at 0635 hours on 7 December, no one in authority showed any interest. Pearl Harbor was wide open to attack.

The midget submarine was, in fact, one of three which approached the American base, acting upon orders received by the entire Japanese force on 2 December, after the Emperor had finally decided that war was unavoidable. The other two entered Pearl Harbor before dawn on 7 December, taking advantage of American neglect to close the torpedo nets across the harbor mouth between 0600 hours and 0840 hours. Meanwhile, Nagumo's force had reached the launching zone, 230 miles due north of Oahu, and the decision to go ahead had been made, despite reports that the American carriers were absent from their usual anchorages. In fact, *Saratoga* was undergoing repairs on the West Coast of the United States, the *Lexington* was ferrying aircraft to Midway in preparation for war, and the *Enterprise* was returning to Pearl Harbor from Wake Island, but with a reported nine battleships, seven cruisers, three submarine-tenders and 20 destroyers at anchor, with no visible defensive screen, the opportunity seemed too good to miss. In the event, the count was not exact – only eight battleships were present and some of the other vessels had been wrongly described – but the discrepancies were minor. Fortunately for the Americans, the absence of carriers was to prove the difference between short-term disaster and long-term defeat.

Fuchida roared off the deck of the *Akagi* at precisely 0600 hours on 7 December, and within 15 minutes the first wave of the attacking force, comprising 43 fighters, 49 high-level bombers, 51 dive bombers and 40 torpedo bombers, had been successfully launched. Following a direct route at approximately 200 mph, the aircraft crossed the Oahu shoreline at 0740 hours to achieve complete surprise. Visibility was excellent, enabling the Japanese airmen to see American fighters and bombers lined up in neat rows in front of their hangars and the fleet at anchor, apparently deserted. Fuchida transmitted the radio message 'Tora, Tora, Tora' – a prearranged code to signify to his superiors in Japan that surprise had been achieved and all was well – and signaled his pilots to follow the first of their practiced plans, whereby the torpedo bombers would go in first, followed by the high-level bombers, leaving the dive bombers and fighters to bring up the rear. As it happened, in the confusion and excitement of the attack, such order rapidly disappeared, but this merely served to add to the surprise and chaos on the ground. At 0755 hours, the first bombs began to fall.

From the beginning of Yamamoto's planning, the fear of a positive American reaction in the air had been uppermost in Japanese minds, particularly when it was estimated that 455 aircraft would be stationed on Oahu at the time of the attack, and for this reason the initial assault was put in against the various Hawaiian airfields. Val dive bombers, with Zero fighter support, concentrated upon Hickam Field and Ford Island, as well as the Wheeler air base. At the latter, American fighters were lined up as if awaiting inspection, and in the first few minutes 20 P-40s and P-36s were destroyed. At Hickam, some 70 bombers – of which 12 were newly-delivered B-17s – were burnt out, and similar pictures emerged at Kaneohe, a flying-boat base, and Ewa, an uncompleted Marine Corps airfield. Within a very short time, American air defense potential had been virtually wiped out – there being, in fact, only 231 aircraft in the Hawaii region – and the Japanese had gained complete air supremacy, enabling the other portions of Fuchida's force to attack the fleet with relative impunity.

The assault upon the battleships began shortly after 0800 hours, with Kate torpedo bombers, divided into two groups, making three successive low, fast runs against minimal opposition. An enormous amount of damage was done. In the first attack the battleships *California*, *Oklahoma* and *West Virginia* were hit; in the second the cruiser *Helena* was struck and the minelayer *Oglala* capsized; in the third the cruiser *Raleigh* and the aged battleship *Utah*, recently used by the Americans as a target ship, were torpedoed. At the same time the dive bombers plummeted down, making eight separate attacks from different points of the compass. Their aim was good – a product of the intense training at Kagoshima Bay – and the results were catastrophic. The battleships *Nevada*, *Maryland*, *Pennsylvania* and *Tennessee* all -caught fire, while the *Arizona*, hit in the forward magazine and boilers, blew up and capsized, showering huge fragments of debris over the harbor. Four hundred seamen were trapped in her upturned hull. Permitting no respite, Fuchida himself led the high-level bombers into the attack, organizing all 49 into a single column and passing over the harbor at 12,000ft. By now the Americans had recovered sufficiently to put up anti-aircraft fire, and as Fuchida's force wheeled round for a second run, two bombers were shot down and a third forced to ram its target. Unperturbed, the bombers made a third and final run, pouring their armor-piercing bombs onto the burning ships, before climbing to 15,000ft and making way for the second wave. It was 0840 hours.

By this time all seven front-line battleships were on fire, and when the second wave of 170 aircraft arrived, led by Lieutenant Commander Shigekazu Shimazaki of the *Zuikaku*, their task was not made easy by billowing clouds of smoke. Nevertheless, a force of 80 Val dive bombers, briefed to hit the absent American carriers, mounted a furious assault upon the battleships, concentrating upon those which were still capable of putting up anti-aircraft fire. The *Nevada* tried to escape by slipping anchor and making for the harbor mouth, but was pounced on and torpedoed in mid-channel. Wallowing dangerously and threatening to sink in the middle of the anchorage, blocking it to all traffic, she had to be nursed to the shore and beached. Meanwhile the high-level bombers of the second wave had revisited the air bases, destroying surviving aircraft and installations at Hickam, Wheeler, Ford Island and Kaneohe. At the latter they were joined by 31 Zero fighters, whose original task of acting as a protective air umbrella had proved unnecessary. At 0945 hours, after nearly two hours sustained assault, the Japanese withdrew.

Fuchida's first wave aircraft reached their carriers at 1000 hours, to be followed two hours later by the last of Shimazaki's force, and when it was found that only 29 machines had been lost of the 353 committed, the pilots were understandably ecstatic, demanding permission to mount another attack. This would have been quite feasible, but Nagumo, worried that the missing American carriers were even then steaming to intercept him, refused. The task force turned for home, transmitting Fuchida's report – 'Four battleships definitely sunk, and considerable damage inflicted on the airfields.' It looked like a crippling blow.

Few people on Oahu at the time would have argued against this assessment. By noon on 7 December eight battleships, three cruisers, three destroyers and eight auxiliary craft – totaling some 300,000 tons – had been immobilized; Hickam, Wheeler, Ford Island and Kaneohe had been destroyed, together with 96 of the 231 aircraft in Hawaii (in fact only seven of the remaining machines were immediately airworthy); and over 3400 people had been killed or wounded. The only success had been against the midget submarines, all of which had been sunk before they could inflict any

damage, but this was minor compared to the sheer shock and force of the Japanese assault. In what looked like a treacherous pre-emptive strike – because of translation problems the actual Japanese severance of negotiations was not delivered to President Roosevelt until after the attack had finished – the US Pacific fleet had been virtually wiped out, enabling the enemy to advance into the Southwest Pacific, free from American interference.

But the Japanese victory was in fact far from complete. The fatal flaw was that the strike had missed the US carriers entirely, so sparing a weapon which was to have decisive effects upon the future conduct of the war. American admirals, denied their traditional dependence upon the battleship, were forced to tear up existing plans and, of necessity, concentrate their attentions upon the role of naval air power. Because the *Saratoga, Enterprise* and *Lexington* escaped Pearl Harbor, the carrier had to replace the battleship as the central feature of fleet organization, rapidly becoming the principal naval weapon. The Americans were quick to learn, using their carriers successfully at the Battles of Coral Sea, Midway, Philippine Sea and the Leyte Gulf to beat the Japanese at their own game. In addition, Fuchida's airmen had failed to destroy the oil tanks, machine shops and other installations on Oahu and, despite the depressing picture on 7 December, Pearl Harbor itself was quick to recover from the blow. Of the eight battleships attacked, all but two were later raised and repaired, as were many of the smaller ships, and in the end the catalog of total destruction contained the names of the *Arizona, Oklahoma* and two destroyers only. Even so, if the lesson provided by Mitchell in 1921 had been heeded, there might have been no need for a catalog at all.

Battleship Row at Pearl Harbor: from left to right are the *Maryland,* the capsized *Oklahoma,* the sunken *West Virginia* burning alongside the *Tennessee.*

2 CORAL SEA
The Balancing Act

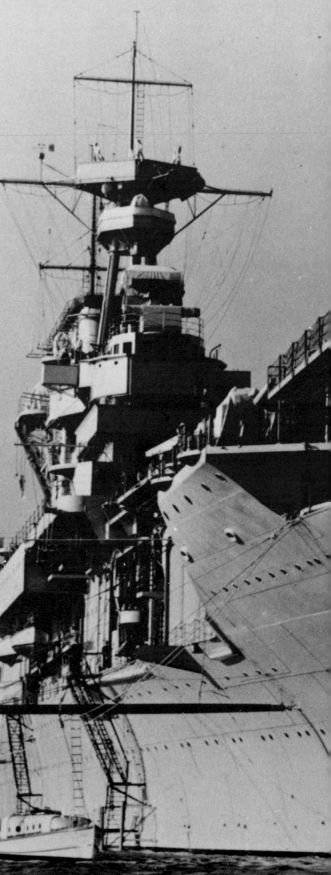

The USS *Yorktown* at Hampton Roads, Virginia on 30 October 1937. The *Yorktown* was Rear Admiral Frank Fletcher's flag ship during Coral Sea.

The Battle of the Coral Sea heralded a revolution in naval warfare. It was the first in which the capital ships of both sides did not so much as catch a glimpse of an opponent. The damage was all done by aircraft, the new artillery of the sea. The battle was one of those, in which the right thing, if it happened at all, usually happened for the wrong reason. It was the first great seafight of the Pacific War, the greatest naval war of all time, fought with, for its prize, the mastery of the Pacific.

The Japanese Navy had not fought a fleet action since Tsushima in 1905. Until January 1936 when Japan had withdrawn from the Washington Naval Limitation Treaty, the details of her naval construction had been known to the Western powers. Thereafter the Japanese went in for a program of naval expansion, but nobody knew precisely what they were building. In fact between 1921 and 1941, while Great Britain and the USA made modest increases to their navies, the Japanese doubled their combat tonnage. By 1941 their navy was more powerful than the Pacific fleets of their opponents, which were not, of course, combined.

The Japanese ships were well designed and well armed. Their fleet was well worked-up, and thoroughly efficient both technically and tactically. The Japanese qualities of discipline, toughness and diligence, were apparent in every department.

Two monster battleships were added in 1940: *Yamato* and *Musashi*, each of 63,000 tons and with 18-inch guns. By that time a comparison of the Japanese and the US Pacific Fleets shows a very considerable advantage to the former.

	Japanese	United States
Battleships	10	9
Carriers	10	3
Heavy cruisers	18	12
Light cruisers	17	9
Destroyers	111	67
Submarines	64	27

32

It is an interesting illustration of the way in which a wealthy democracy, while knowing who its potential opponents are, can allow itself to be outstripped in those warlike preparations, which guarantee peace.

Admiral Isoroku Yamamoto had been interested in naval air warfare since the 1920s, indeed he was the leading light in the small group of officers, who believed in aircraft, and perceived that the days of the battleship were numbered. It takes real courage to peer into the future and predict that a well-loved 'weapon' is obsolescent. Yamamoto was appointed commandant of a naval school, and he supervised the training of many pilots. This is not to say that his views appealed to the more conservative Japanese admirals, who successfully resisted reform of the fleet as a whole. At

Rear Admiral Frank 'Black Jack' Fletcher who was in command of Task Force 17.

the same time, arriving at a typically Japanese solution, they formed an extra and separate fleet oriented toward air tactics. This development went unnoticed by the intelligence services of the Western Powers. It was thought that there were few skilled Japanese naval pilots – an illusion which was shattered at Pearl Harbor.

The Japanese Navy, as we have seen was conservative in its views. The Army on the other hand had involved Japan in its tremendous Chinese adventure, and was in any case deeply involved in the government. With Pearl Harbor the Navy too became involved, though Yamamoto himself had only consented to war because economic sanctions had rendered Japan's position so desperate. With the spread of the war to Southeast Asia and the South Pacific the Japanese Navy had its own theater in which it was paramount. Yamamoto's plan had been to destroy the US fleet at Pearl Harbor, before it could sail and attack the Japanese in the Western Pacific. Oddly

enough the Japanese had not concealed the fact that they did not exclude such an attack from their plans, but with well-nigh incredible complacency the United States had ignored the possibility. It is not generally known, moreover, that the Japanese had given the Americans 30 minutes warning of the attack, an attempt to observe the usages of war, but the message had not got through. Yamamoto's six carriers had put the American battleships out of action, but by a great stroke of good fortune three carriers, which were out on an exercise, had escaped undamaged.

The Japanese, as it turned out, now had two years in which to consolidate their position, or to make peace. By the spring of 1942 they had taken Wake Island, Guam, Hong Kong, the Philippines, Malaya, the Dutch East Indies and most of Burma. Resistance had, generally speaking, been ineffectual, occasionally, as at Singapore, quite inept. Their casualties had been light, and the Japanese became so elated that there seemed no limit to their potential

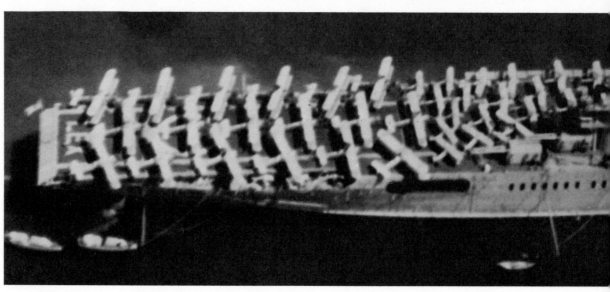

conquests. A second offensive was decided upon.

The proposed strategy of this new campaign may be summarized as follows. The Japanese would first seize Tulagi in the Solomon Islands and Port Moresby in Papua (New Guinea). This would give them air control over the Coral Sea. The Japanese Combined Fleet would then sail on across the Pacific to seek out and destroy what remained of the US Pacific Fleet, besides capturing Midway and the Western Aleutians. They would consolidate their conquests by a 'ribbon defense,' with impregnable fortresses on Attu, Midway, Wake, the Marshalls and the Gilberts. The invasion of New Caledonia, the Fiji Islands and Samoa would isolate Australia and New Zealand. It was felt that, with their fleet destroyed and the ribbon defense established, the Americans would tire of the war and come to terms.

This strategy had been conceived as early as 1938, and formed part of the Japanese Basic War Plan. In 1942 the timetable was speeded up, and the major fleet action with the Americans was added.

Easy successes had given the Japanese a contempt for the Americans. They had become infected, as the perceptive and intelligent Rear Admiral Chuichi Hara was to admit after the war, with 'victory disease.' It is always a mistake to underrate the enemy, and now the Japanese were falling into this error. Moreover, Japan's resources were simply inadequate for the manifold tasks her strategy imposed. The Japanese merchant navy had neither the tonnage nor the organization to supply her far-flung outposts. Nor had Japan the industrial capacity, or even the manpower, to build up a fleet sufficient to protect her long lines of communication. For sea power, as she herself proved, now meant carrier-borne air forces. And her early successes, due to superior pilots, planes and techniques, had not been won without loss. It is estimated that by April 1942 Japan had lost 855 naval planes, 315 in combat

Above: Rear Admiral William Halsey, commander of Task Force 16, the carriers *Hornet* and *Enterprise*. He could not take part in the Battle of Coral Sea because his carrier force was somewhere in the Central Pacific to launch the Doolittle Raid against Japan.

Left: The Japanese carrier, *Shokaku*, seen at Yokosuka on 23 August 1941. She was part of the Carrier Strike Force at Coral Sea, under Vice-Admiral Takeo Takagi.

Left: The USS *Lexington* with a complement of aircraft during the 1920s.

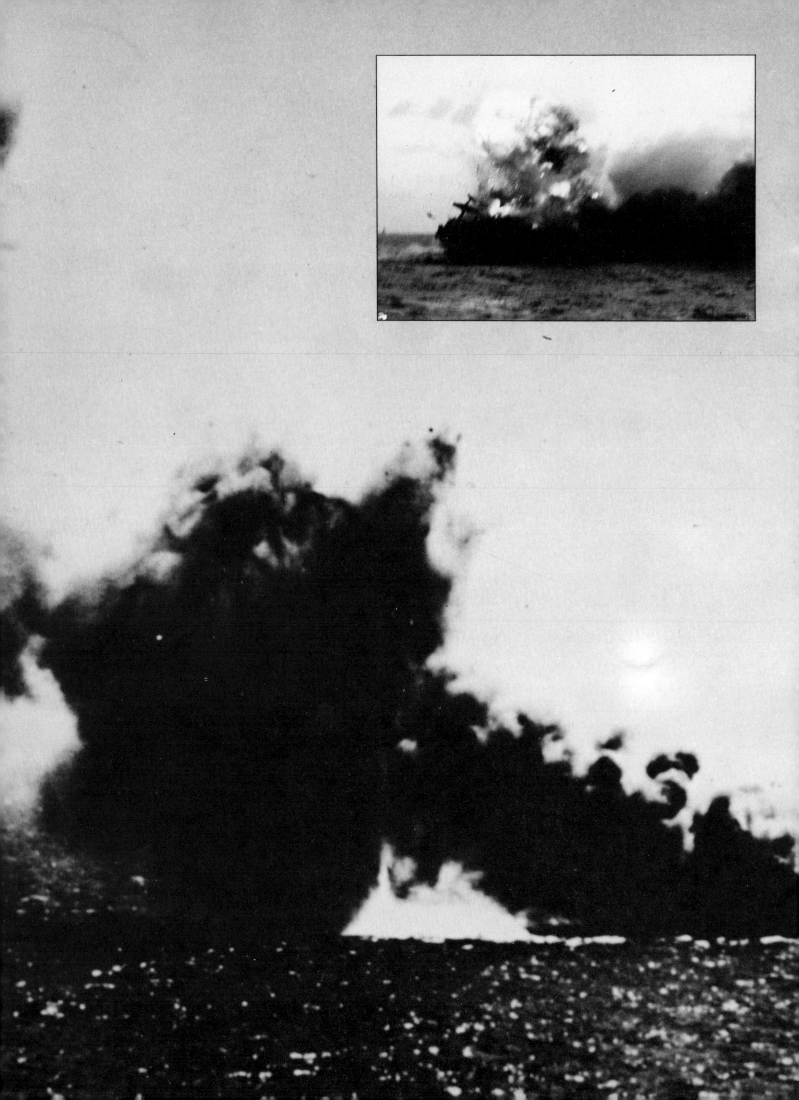

and 540 lost 'operationally.' These losses, were of course, replaced, but there was a decided fall in the quality of air crews. That Yamamoto was right to insist that the US Pacific Fleet must be destroyed by 1943 is certain. He knew very well that the United States with its tremendous economic and industrial capability could outbuild Japan. But would this second offensive overstrain Japan's military potential? That was the question.

In April 1942 the Japanese made a foray into the Indian Ocean, which effectually neutralized the small British forces in those waters. This done they turned their attention to the first objective of the new strategy. The Coral Sea is bounded on one side by New Caledonia, the New Hebrides and the Louisiades, on the other by the Great Barrier Reef.

The Coral Sea was vital to Australian security. Early in the year the Japanese had established a big base at Rabaul, from which the operation was to be mounted.

The Japanese believed that the Americans had only one carrier in the South Pacific. They thought up a complicated plan in which five forces, following different routes, but adhering to a set timetable would surprise the enemy and engage them in an unequal fight. What they did not know was that American intelligence had actually broken their codes before the war, and could decipher many of their fleet messages. By 17 April the American Pacific Fleet had already unraveled the outline of the Japanese plan.

Vice-Admiral Inouye, Commander in Chief of the Fourth Fleet, was the overall commander. It was hoped that with Port Moresby in their hands Japanese aircraft could attack Australian ports and airfields, and perhaps even compel Australia to quit the war.

Left below: The small carrier *Shoho* is torpedoed by the US Navy during the Battle of Coral Sea on 7 May 1942.

Far left: The *Lexington* suffers an internal explosion which got out of control and she had to be abandoned and scuttled on 8 May 1942.

Left: The *Lexington* under air attack during the Battle of Coral Sea.

Operation Mo: Coral Sea
Overall Commander: Vice-Admiral Shigeyoshi Inouye

Groups	Ships	Commander
Port Moresby Invasion Group	11 transports	Rear Admiral Tanaka
Tulagi Invasion Group: set up seaplane base		Rear Admiral Shima
Covering Group: for Tulagi Group and then Port Moresby	Light carrier *Shoho* 4 heavy cruisers 1 destroyer	Rear Admiral Goto
Support Group: establish seaplane base in the Louisiades	2 light cruisers seaplane tender	Rear Admiral Marushige
Striking Force	Carriers *Shokaku* *Zuikaku* 2 heavy cruisers 6 destroyers	Vice-Admiral Takagi
Task Force 17	Carrier *Yorktown*, etc	Rear Admiral Frank Fletcher
Task Force 11	Carrier *Lexington*, etc	Rear Admiral Aubrey Fitch
Task Force 44	2 Australian cruisers 1 American cruiser 2 Destroyers	Rear Admiral Crace, RN

The Mitsubishi A6M5 Zero. This was the improved version of the Zero, which was in action from the autumn of 1943. The Zeros were carrier-based fighters which at first could outpace US fighters, but the F4U Corsair and F6F Hellcat, introduced in 1943 mastered them.

Port Moresby was vital to General Douglas MacArthur's plans. It was to be the major air base from which he would counter the Japanese threat to Australia, and a springboard for his return to the Philippines.

Admiral Chester Nimitz, Commander in Chief of the Pacific Fleet, concentrated all available forces to foil Inouye's threat.

Fletcher was to be the overall Allied commander. Task Force 17 was already in the South Pacific; Task Force 11 was sent from Pearl Harbor. Task Force 44 was what was called 'MacArthur's Navy.' Fletcher's three forces put together were somewhat inferior to Inouye's fleet, if only because the latter had one more carrier, albeit a small one, *Shoho*.

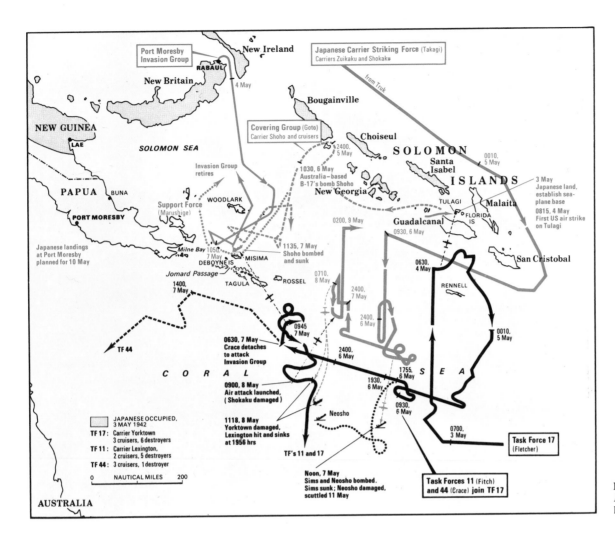

Below: Fires on board the *Lexington* rage shortly after all hands have abandoned ship.

American strategy at this juncture was defensive. Its object was to protect the Hawaiian Islands and communications with Australia and New Zealand via Palmyra, Samoa, Fiji and New Caledonia. MacArthur was organizing the few Australian and American troops of South West Pacific Command for the defense of Papua and northern Australia.

MacArther, who had an impressive record from World War I, and had been Chief of Staff of the US Army, had been on loan to the Philippine Commonwealth at the outbreak of World War II, and had commanded the futile attempt to save the Philippines. It would be idle to pretend that he saw eye to eye with President Roosevelt, or with General Marshall, the Army Chief of Staff. But their differences were as nothing compared to the intense rivalry which quickly sprang up between Mac-Arthur and Nimitz, a rivalry which, for ill or good, was to affect the whole strategy of the

Left: A destroyer comes alongside the *Lexington*, which is listing to port, to take off survivors.

Pacific War. That MacArthur was 'difficult' there can be no question. President Truman was to find that during the Korean War, but where his relations with the US Navy were concerned all the blame cannot be laid at MacArthur's door. The Navy had an ethos all its own. At a time when the United States was pursuing its foreign policy of isolation, the US Navy, self-sufficient and self-contained, was pursuing its own similar policy; secure in the knowledge that it had its own air force, and a Private Army, the US Marine Corps, the élite of the American fighting men. In war the enemy was only marginally more hostile than the army with which the US Navy so reluctantly co-operated! Rivalry between services is not altogether unhealthy: in this case it had been carried rather too far.

1 May
Shima set sail from Rabaul.

Task Forces 11 and 17 rendezvoused north of new Caledonia.

2 May
Reconnaissance plane sighted Shima's force. but the reports which reached Fletcher were not clear. So Fletcher moved northwest with Task Force 17.

Then the Japanese were sighted approaching Tulagi, from which island the small Australian garrison withdrew.

3 May
In the evening, one of MacArthur's reconnaissance planes reported Japanese disembarking on Tulagi. Fletcher in the *Yorktown* made for Tulagi.

4 May
A dawn strike on Tulagi by over 40 American planes sank one destroyer, three small mine sweepers and destroyed five seaplanes. Inexperienced pilots gave glowing reports of this modest score. Fletcher moved south to rendezvous with Fitch. Crace joined Fitch. Takagi's carriers, delivering nine fighters to Rabaul, were still out of range, far from Coral Sea.

5 May
Fletcher concentrated his task forces, and refueled from the tanker *Neosho*. Reconnaissance reports produced a confused picture. Fletcher decided in the evening to set course northwest toward the probable route of the Port Moresby Invasion Force.

Takagi's Carrier Striking Force rounded San Cristobal and turned northwest into the Coral Sea. Neither admiral had any real idea of the size and position of his opponent's fleet.

6 May
Awaiting intelligence Fletcher turned southeast while refueling. In the morning, Takagi set a southerly course, which he hoped would bring him into contact with Fletcher, but he did not send out any reconnaissance planes! A plane from Rabaul spotted Fletcher's force, but this report did not reach Takagi until the next day. American reconnaissance, due to low cloud, failed to locate Takagi, who was only 70 miles from Fletcher's task force.

7 May
Takagi launched an air search at dawn, when he and Fletcher were some 200 miles apart. At 0736 hours, a report reached Takagi of one carrier and one cruiser, 200 miles south-south-west. Takagi thought this was the *only* US carrier in the South Pacific, and launched a major strike: 36 Val dive bombers, 24 Kate torpedo bombers, 18 Zeros as cover. The target turned out to be the tanker *Neosho* and the destroyer *Sims*, which were duly sunk. Reconnaissance planes from one of Goto's cruiser's reported the true position of the American carriers. Fletcher decided to detach Crace, who was to wait south of the Jomard Passage in

	Lexington	Yorktown	Totals
Dauntless dive bombers	28	25	53
Devastator torpedo bombers	12	10	22
Wildcat fighters	10	8	18
	50	43	93

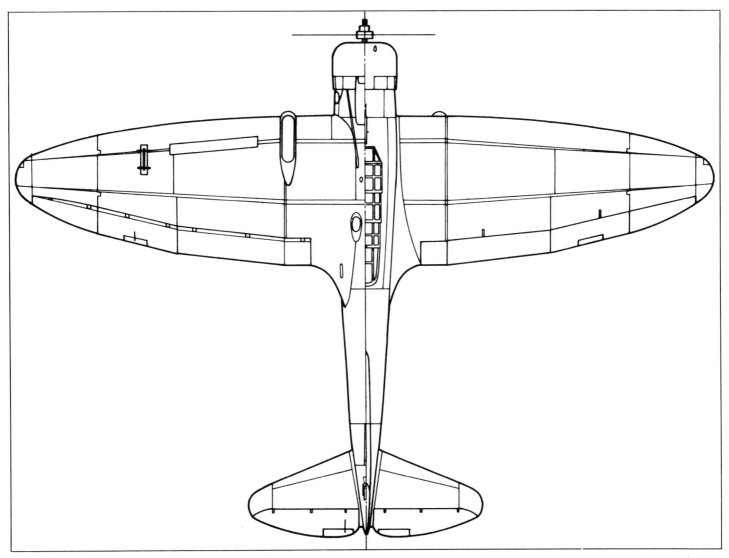

order to block the route of the invasion convoy. The American carriers turned north and launched a major air search, but the Japanese fleet was still concealed by bad weather. By 0815 hours, planes from the *Yorktown* accidentally reported two heavy cruisers and two destroyers as two carriers and four heavy cruisers 175 miles northwest of the American force. (This was actually Marushige's support group.) Fletcher assumed, not unreasonably, that this was the main Japanese force and launched a major strike.

Thus, like Takagi, Fletcher had sent a major strike against a minor target, and was himself vulnerable to shore- or carrier-based attack. Another plane reported a Japanese carrier and other ships in the same target area, so Fletcher did *not* recall his strike (This second force was Goto's covering group, protecting the Port Moresby Invasion Force.) At 1100 hours, attack groups from the *Lexington* sighted Goto

and attacked the *Shoho* by dive bombing from 18,000ft. Japanese Combat Air Patrol shot down one Dauntless, and lost eight fighters. The *Shoho* was sunk in ten minutes, and the strike leader signaled: 'Scratch one flattop.'

At 1338 hours, the *Lexington*'s force returned from their mission having lost three planes. Admiral Inouye at his headquarters in Rabaul, informed of Crace's position, and of the loss of the *Shoho*, ordered Shima to hold the Port Moresby Invasion Force at a safe distance north of the Louisiades, so Goto followed Shima. In a mix-up over identification three of MacArthur's B-17s from Townville, Queensland, attacked Crace, who managed to beat them off!

Then Task Force 44 came under attack from 31 Japanese shore-based bombers, but Crace handled his ships brilliantly, and not one was hit. The Japanese reported the destruction of two battleships and a heavy cruiser.

The Aichi D3A Val was the standard carrier based fighter of the Japanese AF during the opening months of the war. The Vals suffered heavy losses during the Battles of Coral Sea and Midway and were consequently phased out to serve with land-based units.

A lifeboat with survivors from the burning *Lexington*.

In the late afternoon Takagi sent out a search-mission: 12 Vals and 15 Kates. (No Zeros as they were not capable of night operations.) The search proving fruitless they jettisoned bombs and torpedoes and made for home. Their course took them over Fletcher's fleet, which got 20 minutes warning from radar. His Combat Air Patrol of Wildcats shot down eight Kates. Vals shot down two Wildcats, for the loss of one.

At dusk, three Japanese aircraft attempted to land on the *Lexington* and three on the *Yorktown*, because they had lost their way. Only seven of the 27 Japanese planes landed safely back on their carriers.

Takagi, after considering an attempt to bring on a night action with his cruisers, decided that with the loss of the *Shoho* he must give the Invasion Force air protection. He turned north. Both admirals now had a good idea of the strength and position of their opponents. Each gave tactical command of his fleet to the most experienced carrier officer of flag rank. These were Aubrey Fitch and Chuichi Hara.

8 May

At the crisis of the battle the two carrier groups were fairly evenly matched:

	Japanese	*United States*
Planes	121	122
Carriers	2	2
Heavy Cruisers	4	5
Destroyers	6	7

Hara decided to launch an early search 200 miles southeast and southwest. At dawn in heavy rain squalls Hara launched a strike force of 33 Vals, 18 Kates and 18 Zeros. It was airborne by the time the air search reported the American force 180 miles south, with its own air search launched.

A reconnaissance plane from the *Lexington* spotted the Japanese fleet soon after.

At 0915 hours, a strike force from the two US carriers made for the Japanese fleet, composed of 46 dive bombers; 21 torpedo bombers and 15 fighters. At 1057 hours 41 planes from the *Yorktown* attacked the *Shokaku*, while the

Zuikaku was hidden in a rain squall. A Dauntless landed a 500lb bomb on the *Shokaku* so that planes could no longer be launched from her flight deck.

The *Lexington's* attack group was disorganized by the rain clouds, and many planes, unable to find the target, turned back. But four Dauntless and 11 Devastators went into the attack, scoring one bomb hit, killing 100 men, and starting a fire in the *Shokaku*. The strike cost the Americans 13 planes: five dive bombers, five torpedo bombers and three fighters.

Meanwhile the Japanese strike force, almost 70 planes, caught the American Combat Air Patrol low on fuel. Despite 20 minutes warning from radar, nine Wildcats did not have the altitude to meet the attack with advantage. The Japanese courageously pressed home their attack against unpracticed American Ack-Ack gunners, in action for the first time. Surrounded by torpedo tracks the *Lexington*, unable to take avoiding action against them all, received two torpedo and two bomb hits. The *Yorktown*, with a shorter turning circle, received a bomb on her flight-deck, which, however, remained serviceable. By noon the battle was over.

The *Yorktown*, with 66 men killed by a single bomb was still in fighting trim, and her planes were still landing. The *Lexington*, listing seven degrees to port, was containing three major fires, but her power plant was intact.

At 1247 hours violent internal explosions shook the *Lexington*, resulting from gasoline fumes and finally threatened the ready bomb storage. The fires soon raged uncontrollably and at 1707 hours orders were given to abandon ship.

Right: Admiral Nimitz awards the Distinguished Service Cross to Admiral Thomas Kinkaid for his action in the Battle of the Coral Sea. Kinkaid was later to play an important part in the Central Pacific advance and in the Battle of Leyte Gulf.

At 1853 hours using five torpedoes, a destroyer sank the *Lexington* with 35 planes still aboard her. Inouye, frightened at the prospect of intensive allied air activity, postponed the Port Moresby invasion, so the Allies had achieved their objective. Takagi withdrew to Truk and then Yamamoto ordered him south to 'annihilate' the remnants of the enemy.

With the Port Moresby invasion foiled Admiral Nimitz ordered Fletcher to withdraw so that the *Yorktown* would be available for the defense of Midway.

Thus the battle ended. It was in terms of profit and loss a draw. Indeed the Japanese had lost the little *Shoho* while the Americans had lost the *Lexington*. The *Yorktown* had to go to Pearl Harbor for repairs, while the *Shokaku*, heavily damaged, had to limp back to Japan for repairs which took two months. The *Zuikaku* had so few planes left that she had to go home for replacements. The Japanese had lost 75 percent of their bomber pilots and planes.

The battle showed that the Japanese pilots were not the men of Pearl Harbor. They were, moreover, unaccustomed to night operations. The Kate was a lumbering old kite and the lack of radar had been a serious disadvantage to the Japanese. Yamamoto was always alert in keeping abreast of technological advances – indeed it is practically a principle of war that one should do so. Still at a time when the despised British had been using radar for two years, and the Germans knew all about it, the Japanese persisted in ignoring it. One could even assert that they could have won this battle had they previously adopted radar. Oddly enough the Germans had sent two radar sets to their ally by submarine. For some reason, lack of technicians perhaps, the Japanese were unimpressed. Co-operation between Germany and Japan was in fact minimal.

So one could say that the Battle of the Coral Sea was a draw. But that is not really so. It was a battle that the Japanese might have been expected to win, but in which the Allies, with their inexperienced pilots, had held their own. Admirals Fletcher, Fitch and Crace had really deserved well of their countries!

The Americans emerged from the ordeal with clearer ideas on the tactical use of carriers. This was, of course, to serve them well at Midway and thereafter. More to the point, Coral Sea marked the high water mark of Japanese southward expansion. It was their first repulse. The level-headed and experienced Yamamoto found in it confirmation of his views that the further acquisition of territory, so far from helping Japan, would merely squander her exiguous resources.

Fortified by the prestige he had won at Pearl Harbor Yamamoto, quite correctly, now convinced his more conservative colleagues, that the paramount object of the Japanese Fleet must be to complete the destruction of the United States Pacific Fleet. This thinking led naturally to the next great battle – Midway.

Coral Sea was a tactical draw, but strategically, it saved Port Moresby, the gateway to New Guinea, and Australia. The relatively good news raised morale, when the fall of Corregidor could have had a really depressing effect in the United States.

Thirty-six years have passed since Fletcher led forth his hastily assembled and relatively untrained force to counter the very serious threat to Port Moresby. It was a heavy responsibility, which he discharged competently against a vigorous foe.

The main interest of Coral Sea, however, is that it ushers in a new era in the history of naval warfare: the paramountcy of the aircraft carrier.

A Douglas SBD Dauntless
dives over a burning
Japanese ship at the height
of the Battle of Midway.

3 MIDWAY
The Turning Point

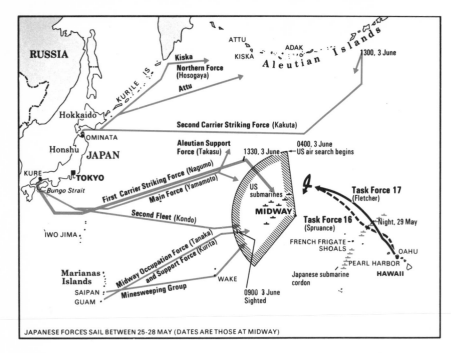

RUSSIA

ATTU
ADAK
Kiska
KISKA
Aleutian Islands
1300, 3 June

KURILE IS.

Northern Force
(Hosogaya)

Attu

Hokkaido

OMINATA

Honshu JAPAN

Second Carrier Striking Force (Kakuta)

Aleutian Support
Force (Takasu)

1330, 3 June

0400, 3 June
US air search begins

KURE TOKYO

Bungo Strait

First Carrier Striking Force (Nagumo)

Main Force (Yamamoto)

US submarines

Task Force 17
(Fletcher)

Second Fleet (Kondo)

MIDWAY

Task Force 16
(Spruance)

Night, 29 May

IWO JIMA

FRENCH FRIGATE
SHOALS

OAHU

Marianas
Islands

Midway Occupation Force (Tanaka)
and Support Force (Kurita)

WAKE

PEARL HARBOR

HAWAII

SAIPAN

Minesweeping Group

Japanese submarine
cordon

GUAM

0900 3 June
Sighted

JAPANESE FORCES SAIL BETWEEN 25-28 MAY (DATES ARE THOSE AT MIDWAY)

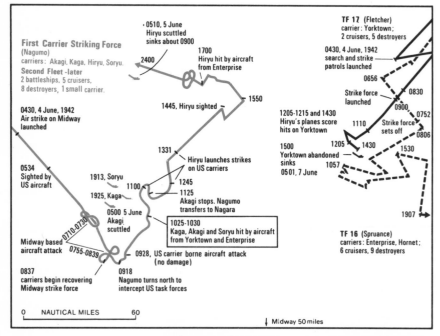

First Carrier Striking Force
(Nagumo)
carriers: Akagi, Kaga, Hiryu, Soryu.
Second Fleet -later
2 battleships, 5 cruisers,
8 destroyers, 1 small carrier.

• 0510, 5 June
Hiryu scuttled
sinks about 0900

1700
Hiryu hit by aircraft
from Enterprise

2400

0430, 4 June, 1942
Air strike on Midway
launched

1445, Hiryu sighted

1550

TF 17 (Fletcher)
carrier: Yorktown;
2 cruisers, 5 destroyers

0430, 4 June, 1942
search and strike
patrols launched

0656

Strike force
launched

0830

0900

0752

1205-1215 and 1430
Hiryu's planes score
hits on Yorktown

1110

Strike force
sets off

0806

0534
Sighted by
US aircraft

1913, Soryu

1331

Hiryu launches strikes
on US carriers

1245

1925, Kaga

1100

1125
Akagi stops. Nagumo
transfers to Nagara

1500
Yorktown abandoned
sinks
0501, 7 June

1205

1430

1530

1057

0500 5 June
Akagi
scuttled

1025-1030
Kaga, Akagi and Soryu hit by aircraft
from Yorktown and Enterprise

1907

Midway based
aircraft attack

0710-0730

0755-0839

0928, US carrier borne aircraft attack
(no damage)

TF 16 (Spruance)
carriers: Enterprise, Hornet;
6 cruisers, 9 destroyers

0837
carriers begin recovering
Midway strike force

0918
Nagumo turns north to
intercept US task forces

0 NAUTICAL MILES 60

Midway 50 miles

Right: Vice-Admiral Chuichi
Nagumo, who was
Commander in Chief of the
Japanese carrier force at
Midway.

Far right: Admiral Isoroku
Yamamoto devised the
Midway operation and
followed the battle from his
flagship, the giant battleship
Yamato.

June 1942

Midway Island is a flyspeck in the vast Pacific
Ocean, about halfway between Pearl Harbor
and Japan. It is, in fact, an atoll – two tiny
islands almost entirely surrounded by a barrier
reef. In the center of the atoll is a lagoon with
a narrow ship channel leading to it, on the
western edge an open harbor. A few insignificant bits of coral – but in June 1942, they were
to become the object of one of the greatest
naval battles of World War II.

Admiral Isoroku Yamamoto, Commander
in Chief of the Japanese Combined Fleet, had
presented his plans for the campaign to the
General Staff at the beginning of April 1942.
It called for luring the remnants of the
American Pacific Fleet to the defense of the
solitary outpost, forcing it into a decisive
battle, and destroying it.

The Naval General Staff agreed that a decisive battle was necessary at that point in the
war, but was not convinced that Midway, only
1136 miles west-northwest of Pearl Harbor, was
the best place to fight it. Instead, many members advocated cutting the lines of communication between the US and Australia by
advancing on the islands of Fiji and Samoa. In
addition, II Fleet objected on the grounds that
it was not ready; IV Fleet, which was detailed
to look after logistical problems following the
occupation of the island, claimed it could not
guarantee its ability to carry out this function
even if the operation was successful; and I Air
Fleet wanted to postpone the campaign to gain
some time for rest and refitting after extensive
operations in the Indian Ocean. Others pointed
out that if the battle took place as planned,
Japan's two most powerful carriers, the *Shokaku*
and *Zuikaku*, would have to be left behind.

But Yamamoto stood firm. One of Japan's greatest military geniuses, with the rare ability both to devise original ideas and translate them into action, he had never been entirely confident about his island country's ability to wage war against an industrial giant like the United States. Before the war he had warned the Premier, General Hideki Tojo, that 'If I am told to fight . . . I shall run wild for the first six months or a year, but I have utterly no confidence for the second and third years.' His outlook was not improved by the success of the Japanese attack on Pearl Harbor; he wrote to his sister, '. . . in spite of all the clamor that is going on we could lose [the war]. I can only do my best.' He now felt that success at Midway was not only vital strategically, but essential to Japan's survival. Eventually the General Staff gave in.

Just at this time, on 18 April, 16 B-25 bombers led by Lieutenant Colonel James Doolittle carried out a surprise attack on Tokyo from the aircraft carriers *Enterprise* and *Hornet*. They inflicted very little physical damage, but the psychological impact of this first attack on the Home Islands themselves was enormous. The Japanese had no idea where the raid came from (Roosevelt's comment that it had come from Shangri-La was not very helpful), and many suspected that it had originated from Midway. To the major goal of the Midway campaign – the destruction of the American fleet and subsequent mastery of the Pacific Ocean – was added another purpose: capture of the island would protect the Emperor from the indignity of being bombed again. It would also mean the elimination of an important refueling base for US submarines and provide a base for future raids on Pearl Harbor.

Left: Admiral Chester Nimitz, Commander in Chief of the US Pacific Fleet, was in charge of US operations at Midway.

Left: Rear Admiral Frank Fletcher, commander of Task Force 17. His flagship was still the *Yorktown*.

Left: Lieutenant General Jimmy Doolittle and Rear Admiral Marc Mitscher on board the USS *Hornet* shortly before the Doolittle raid.

47

On 5 May, then, Imperial General Headquarters issued the order: 'Commander in Chief Combined Fleet will, in co-operation with the Army, invade and occupy strategic points in the Western Aleutians and Midway Island.'

By that time the first phase in the great Japanese offensive – the campaign to achieve control of the Coral Sea by seizing Tulagi in the Solomon Islands and Port Moresby in Papua – was well underway. The Battle of the Coral Sea, which began on 8 May, was a portent of the trend in naval battles. For the first time in history, two fleets fought at a range of more than a hundred miles, without ever seeing each other. It was aircraft carrier against aircraft carrier while the great obsolete battleships proved to be of little use.

The opposing forces in that battle were more or less evenly matched; the Japanese V Carrier Division under Rear Admiral Chuichi Hara contained the two carriers *Shokaku* and *Zuikaku*, while Task Forces 17 and 11 contained the two American carriers *Lexington* and *Yorktown*. Tactically, the action could be called a draw. The Japanese sank one heavy carrier – the *Lexington* – and heavily damaged *Yorktown*. On the other hand the Americans did achieve their aim of preventing the occupation of Port Moresby and, in addition, gained good experience in the tactical use of carriers. The Americans inflicted their share of damage as well: the *Shokaku* was so badly damaged that she was forced to retire for two months for repairs, while the *Zuikaku* lost so many crews and planes that she too had to return to Japan to be

refitted. Overall, the Japanese pilots showed themselves unused to night operations and not all up to the high standards demonstrated at Pearl Harbor; over three-quarters of their bombing planes and pilots were lost. But the setback in the Battle of the Coral Sea – the first the Japanese had suffered – confirmed Yamamoto in his belief that top priority had to be given to the destruction of the rest of the American Fleet. Thus, the stage was set for the Midway campaign.

Yamamoto's battle plan, modeled on Hannibal's strategy at Cannae and Ludendorff's at Tannenberg, was a complicated one, utilizing the diversionary tactics and division of forces that were always integral parts of Japanese strategy. The standard Japanese pattern was to lure the enemy into an unfavorable tactical position, cut off his retreat, drive in on his flanks, and then concentrate forces for the kill.

Midway was no exception; Yamamoto's plan called for a strike on 3 June against Dutch Harbor in the Aleutians. Destruction of the American base and occupation of the western islands would not only secure the northernmost anchors of Japan's proposed 'ribbon defense,' but would, he hoped, lure the US Pacific Fleet northward. While the Americans were rushing to defend the Aleutians the Japanese would bomb and occupy Midway by 5 June. Then when the American fleet returned, before 7 June, Japanese planes based

Below: The USS *Enterprise* makes its way to Midway Island shortly before the battle.

on the island and on carriers would mount an intensive bombing offensive. Any ships that escaped would be sunk by the Japanese battleships and cruisers.

Surprise was the key element in Yamamoto's plan; there was to be no challenge from the Americans until after Midway had been occupied. Even if the enemy did not take up the Aleutian challenge, they could not get to Midway before 7 June. And even if they did not contest the occupation, the pressure from Midway on Pearl Harbor would soon force them to counterattack.

The Japanese force was divided into five sections. An Advance Force of 16 submarines would harass the Americans as they approached Midway from either the Aleutians or Pearl Harbor. The Northern Area Force under Vice-Admiral Hosogaya consisted of the light carriers *Ryujo* and *Junyo*, along with two heavy cruisers, a destroyer screen, and four transport ships carrying troops for occupying the Aleutian islands of Adak, Attu, and Kiska.

The most power lay with Vice-Admiral Chuichi Nagumo's Main Striking Force: the four big carriers *Akagi*, *Kaga*, *Hiryu*, and *Soryu*, and their screen of destroyers and cruisers. Nagumo's task was to launch air strikes against Midway, to soften it up for Admiral Nobutake Kondo's Midway Occupation Force. Kondo had two battleships, six heavy cruisers, and many destroyers to support the 12 transports carrying a 5000-man occupation force.

Yamamoto was 300 miles behind Nagumo and Kondo, with the Main Body – a force composed of nine battleships and two light carriers, with their attendant cruiser and destroyer screen. He was flying his flag in the newly-constructed *Yamato* which, with its nine 18-inch guns, was the biggest and most powerful battleship in the world. There was little chance that the battleships, with a maximum range of only 40 miles, would play much part in the battle; some of Nagumo's younger officers claimed caustically that the battleship fleet was holding a naval review in the Pacific.

Left: Grumman F4F fighters taking off from the *Enterprise* off Midway.

But Yamamoto, despite the great importance that he gave to aircraft and carriers, still felt it necessary to compromise with the conservatives who still advocated big ships and big guns.

The Japanese Fleet contained almost the entire fighting force of the Japanese Navy – 162 ships including four heavy carriers, four light carriers, 11 battleships, 22 cruisers, 65 destroyers, and 21 submarines.

To counter the blow that Yamamoto was planning, the Americans had three carriers – the *Enterprise*, *Hornet*, and *Yorktown*, eight cruisers, and 15 destroyers. There were no battleships; they rested on the bottom of Pearl Harbor, except for a few stationed on the West Coast that were too old and too slow to be of any real use in modern warfare. But even that small force was more than Yamamoto had thought the Americans could assemble. He believed that the *Yorktown* had been sunk in the Battle of the Coral Sea along with the *Lexington*, when in fact she had managed somehow to limp back to Pearl Harbor. Much has been made of the fact that the carrier was repaired and reprovisioned in three days and three nights, when the job would normally have taken 90 days. But it would be far from accurate to imply that the repairs were anything other than rough jury-rigging. The hull was patched and damaged compartments were braced with timbers. But only a few of the watertight doors were fixed and three superheated boilers that had been knocked out were not even touched. The ship would never be able to make a speed better than 27 knots.

The island of Midway itself served as a base for 54 Marine Corps planes (including 25 obsolete Brewster Buffalo fighters), 32 Navy Catalinas, and 23 Air Force planes (including 17 B-17s and six brand new Navy Avenger torpedo bombers). In addition to its planes, the island had two good search radars, was dotted with artillery, and had almost 3000 men in Army and Marine units dug in and protected by bombproof shelters throughout the island. The actual invasion never took place, but if it had there is no certainty it would have succeeded. Midway's defenses were as carefully prepared as Tarawa's would be later in the war, and Kondo's force of 5000 was not nearly as impressive as the American force that eventually took Tarawa.

Admiral Chester Nimitz, Commander in Chief of the Pacific Fleet, was the man charged with containing the Japanese threat. Nimitz was a 57-year-old Texan who had served in a variety of commands, including a stint in the submarine service during World War I, since his graduation from the US Naval Academy. He had made Rear Admiral in 1938, had been promoted to admiral in 1941, and was given command of the Pacific Fleet following the raid on Pearl Harbor. His calm, confident manner and refusal to bring in new staff gradually rebuilt shattered morale, and even with the meager forces at his disposal he was able to organize raids on Japanese bases in the Marshall Islands, New Guinea, and New Britain during the spring of 1942.

Rear Admiral Frank Jack Fletcher, the spare, leathery veteran of the Coral Sea, was in tactical command of the forces mustered to defend Midway. Fletcher – 'Black Jack Fletcher' to his men, though his hair was blond and his eyes blue – was the commander of Task Force 17 built around the patched-up *Yorktown*. He had no control over the Midway-based forces, the submarines operating in the area, or the force sent to defend the Aleutians. Nor did he exercise much control over Task Force 16, which was centered on the *Enterprise* and the *Hornet*, under the temporary command of Rear Admiral Raymond Spruance; Rear Admiral William Halsey (mistakenly nicknamed 'Bull' by a confused journalist) was in the hospital being treated for a skin disease.

In one sense Yamamoto had done the US Navy a favor at Pearl Harbor by effectively forcing America into the new age of carrier warfare. Although in 1941 the Navy was still wedded to the notion that battleships and big guns engaging in epic Jutland-style battles constituted naval warfare, they were forced by the destruction of Battleship Row to make full and exclusive use of their real power – the carriers and the fighter planes, with their bombs and airborne torpedoes. Nimitz and his subordinate officers were adept at meeting the new situation, while Yamamoto had to contend with the highly conservative staff of the Japanese Navy, many of whom found his interest in naval air warfare anathema.

With the vast area of the Central and South Pacific to defend and with only modest forces at his disposal, Nimitz would have found him-

Left: Douglas SBD Dauntlesses sweep down over Midway on a mission against Japanese carriers.

Crewmen relax during a lull. They are sitting on the mount of a 5-inch gun on board the *Yorktown*.

self in difficulties many times had not American intelligence come to his aid. The Japanese codes had been broken long before the war started, and as a result the Pacific Command usually had enough information from decoded fleet messages to form a reasonably accurate picture of Japanese intentions.

By 10 May intelligence had already confirmed Nimitz's suspicions about the next Japanese objective – Midway. He even had the major details of Yamamoto's plan, along with his approximate schedule and routes. Nimitz was familiar enough with Yamamoto's philosophy and style to predict a full attack on the island, with the destruction of the American carriers as one of the primary objectives, even though some of his officers feared that it was all an elaborate deception designed to cover another attack on Pearl Harbor or the West Coast.

The North Pacific Task Force – two heavy cruisers, three light cruisers, a destroyer division, a nine-destroyer strike group, six S-Class submarines, and numerous other craft – was formed by 17 May and placed under the command of Rear Admiral Robert ('Fuzzy') Theobald. Theobald did not get to Kodiak, off the Alaskan coast, to take command until 27 May, however; and the main body of his fleet was still assembling when the Japanese attacked Dutch Harbor on 3 June.

Meanwhile, on 24 May, Fletcher received a high-priority, top secret message at Tongatabu in the Friendly Islands where he was refueling and repairing what damage he could after his pounding on the Coral Sea. 'What it said,' he later recalled, 'was simply this: Get the hell back here, quick.' Fletcher hoisted anchor almost immediately; 26 May marked the *Yorktown*'s hundredth day at sea without proper replenishment – a record unequaled by any other modern American warship up to that time – and on 27 May she was steaming up the channel to Pearl Harbor to the accompaniment of whistles, sirens, and cheers. On 28 May the *Hornet* and *Enterprise* left to take up their stations; *Yorktown* followed on 30 May. Fletcher and Spruance had received their orders: to '... inflict maximum damage on the enemy by employing strong attrition attacks' (in other words, heavy air strikes). A further letter of instruction directed them to be 'governed by the principles of calculated risk.'

Nagumo's Japanese carrier force left their home base on 26 May, followed by Yamamoto and the Main Body on 28 May. Neither commander was feeling very happy; Yamamoto was suffering from stomach cramps caused by tension, and Nagumo was worried because his carriers and crew had had barely a month for maintenance and refresher training. He later commented, 'We participated in the battle with meager training and without knowledge of the enemy.' Morale among the men in the fleet was high, however. Meanwhile, Japanese submarines were taking up stations east of Midway to intercept any American ships sent out to relieve the island.

As they approached Midway from the west the Japanese Main Striking Force was shielded from patrolling American search planes by the many storms and fogs that occur in that area in May and June. Aboard his flagship, the carrier *Akagi*, Nagumo went over his plans for the last time. He decided to send 100 planes against Midway on 4 June and to hold back an equal number, including some torpedo planes, for a second wave. Of his many long-range scouts, which included cruiser and battleship float planes with a range of over 600 miles, seven would be detailed to keep a lookout for an enemy task force while Midway was being hit. They would cover an arc from due south to northeast; in the unlikely event that an American force should appear, the second wave could be sent against it instead of against the island.

Starting on 30 May, Nimitz began taking precautions to ensure against a Japanese sneak attack. The 22 Navy Catalina patrol bombers on Midway were sent on daily sweeps 700 miles out, and the Midway B-17s flew on daily search-attack missions to the area where the enemy was expected.

The waddling Catalinas were both the joy and despair of American pilots. They climbed, flew, and landed at almost the same speed (about 65 knots) and were armed only with .30 caliber machine guns in side blisters. The rumbling amphibians were death traps when cornered by Japanese fighters, but their redeeming feature was that they could fly almost almost all day long without refueling.

Just before noon on 2 June Task Forces 16 and 17 – the *Yorktown* and her escorts, and the *Enterprise*, *Hornet* and their escorts – rendez-

Above: A Douglas SBD Dauntless ditches into the sea by a heavy cruiser after it has run out of gas.

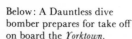

Below: A Dauntless dive bomber prepares for take off on board the *Yorktown*.

occupied by the Japanese by 7 June, but the Army P-40s on Unmak convinced Hosogaya to bypass that island.

At 0843 hours the first sighting report was received from a Midway-based Catalina pilot, who continued to shadow the 11 Japanese ships he had found until 1100 hours. Fletcher concluded rightly that they were not the large carrier force he was expecting; in fact, they were probably Kondo's Midway Occupation Force. Nine Army B-17s took off from Midway to attack the convoy, but made no hits. Fletcher, who was 300 miles east-northeast of Midway (and some 400 miles east of Nagumo), was certain that the Japanese carriers would approach the island from the northwest and strike the following day. Assuming that his presence was – and would remain – unknown, he hoped to be in a position to launch an attack against the carriers from their left flank as soon as the enemy planes had begun their strike against Midway. At 1931 hours on 3 June, he altered course to the southwest, which would bring him to a point some 200 miles north of Midway by morning. Through the night of 3–4 June the two carrier forces sailed toward each other on converging courses.

At 0430 hours on the morning of 4 June, 15 minutes after some 11 Catalinas had taken off from Midway to make another attempt to find

voused at 'Point Luck' about 325 miles northeast of Midway, and Fletcher took command of the combined fleet.

The Battle of Midway opened at 0300 hours on 3 June, more than 1000 miles from the atoll itself, with the diversionary attack in the Aleutians. Theobald had deployed his force 400 miles south of Kodiak, fearing an attack on the American base at Dutch Harbor. Hosogaya's force slipped by the Americans easily in the fog and rain, however, and the base in the Eastern Aleutians was heavily bombed. The undefended islands of Attu and Kiska were

the Japanese carriers, the *Yorktown* sent up ten dive bombers on a 100-mile search, as a routine precaution against the possibility of surprise. At the same time, 215 miles to the west, Nagumo was launching his first strike against Midway: 36 Nakajima B5N2s (Kates), 36 Aichi D3A2s (Vals), and 36 Mitsubichi A6M3s (Zeros) rose from the decks of their four carriers. At 0500 hours the 108 Japanese planes were in formation, flying on a steady course for Midway.

Along with this first strike wave, Nagumo also sent up seven float planes to make a 300-mile reconnaissance. But no one in command really expected the American fleet to be anywhere near the area, and their overconfidence must have been transmitted to the search planes. Even though a seaplane from the heavy cruiser *Chikuma* passed almost directly over the US force and had an indecisive encounter with one of the *Yorktown*'s Dauntless dive bombers, it failed to either spot the American ships or to report the engagement, which would have been a sure sign of the presence of an American aircraft carrier in the vicinity.

At 0530 hours one of the Catalina pilots spotted the Japanese carriers through the heavy cloud cover and radioed a report back to Midway; the message was intercepted by the *Enterprise* and relayed to Fletcher on *Yorktown* at 0534 hours. A few minutes later, at 0545 hours, a second PBY radioed another message, without even bothering with code: 'Many planes headed Midway, repeat, Midway . . . .' The pilot then continued to shadow the Japanese ships, dodging the fighters that had been sent up to intercept him, until he was joined by other Catalinas who kept the carriers under constant surveillance from then on.

As soon as Fletcher had an approximate position for the Japanese force he signaled Spruance to proceed southwest with the *Enterprise* and *Hornet* and 'attack the enemy carriers when definitely located.' The *Yorktown* would wait to recover her search planes and obtain further information. At the same time (about 0530 hours) every plane on Midway was being ordered into the air in response to the Catalina's warning; by 0600 hours the only plane left on the ground was an old Grumman single-float biplane. Most of the interceptors were elderly, slow, Marine Corps Buffaloes – no match for the efficient new Zeros. But anti-

aircraft fire on the island was good and about a third of the Japanese strike force was shot down. They had inflicted a fair amount of damage on the ground installations – barracks, mess halls, oil tanks, even the hospital. But casualties were light and the runways remained useable. Six new Navy Avenger torpedo bombers and four Army B-26s streaked after the recent attackers to counterattack, and 16 B-17s already in the air were also ordered to turn north and attack the Japanese carriers.

Nagumo's second strike force (93 planes) was waiting on its flight decks, armed with bombs and torpedoes, in case enemy surface forces appeared. But the returning planes from the first strike reported that the island would require another attack – a point that was emphasized by the appearance of the ten American planes from Midway even though they were not able to score a hit.

At 0715 hours Nagumo ordered the second wave planes taken below and rearmed with incendiary and fragmentation bombs for an attack on the island, clearing the decks for the return of the first wave; the entire process would take about an hour. Although in retrospect the order appears to have been a colossal blunder, at the time it seemed a reasonable move; Japanese scout planes had found no sign of an American surface force in the area, and Midway obviously had to be struck again since planes from the island had just attacked Nagumo's own ship.

But not quite 15 minutes later, at 0728 hours, the Admiral was amazed to receive the worst

The Japanese aircraft carrier *Hiryu* burns during the Battle of Midway. It was aircraft from the *Hiryu* which damaged the *Yorktown*. The *Hiryu* was hit by a dive-bomber attack from the *Enterprise* and *Hornet*. Despite strenuous firefighting she had to be abandoned in the morning and eventually sank at 0900 on 6 June 1942.

Above: A Nakajima B5N
Kate flying over the USS
Yorktown, which is almost
dead in the water following
a torpedo hit.

Right: A Japanese torpedo
scores a direct hit on the
Yorktown.

Right: Heavy smoke rises
from the stack of the *Yorktown*.

Right: By 1500 hours the
Yorktown had developed a
26 degree list to port.

possible news from the *Chikuma's* scout plane –
a vague report that an 'estimated ten ships'
had been sighted in the northeast. Nagumo
paced the bridge for another 15 minutes, then
asked the reconnaissance plane for more
specific information and ordered the second
planes to be rearmed with torpedoes. At 0809
hours the scout plane reported that the enemy
force consisted of five cruisers and five destroyers; at 0820 hours the pilot added that they
were accompanied by 'what appears to be a
carrier' (the *Yorktown*). Nagumo's worst fears
had been realized, but he could not send his
second wave off; the flight decks had to be kept
clear to recover the first Midway strike force.

Following the first attack by the Avengers
and B-26s the Japanese carrier force had been
subjected to a series of attacks, first by the
Army B-17s, then by a flight of 11 old Vought
SB2U Vindicators piloted by Marines, and
finally by the submarine *Nautilus*, which had
intercepted early reports of the Japanese
position. Without fighter cover, however, all
the planes were beaten off without scoring a
single hit and the submarine was only able to
fire one ineffective torpedo before she had to
run for her life under a heavy Japanese depth
charge attack. At this point Nagumo had been
attacked by 52 American planes and one submarine, and had not been touched; his fleet
was intact while over half of the aircraft on
Midway had been knocked out. As far as he
knew he had only to launch one more strike at
Midway and deal with one American carrier,
but Spruance had already decided on a strategy
and launched his own attack forces.

Spruance had originally intended waiting
until 0900 hours when he would be about 100
miles from the enemy, but after discussions
with his Chief of Staff, Captain Miles Browning, he decided to launch his planes early in
hopes of catching the carriers while the Japanese attack planes were being rearmed and refueled. He sent up almost every operational
plane he had – 67 Dauntless dive bombers, 29
torpedo bombers, and 20 Wildcats – holding
back only 32 Wildcats for combat air patrol.
The pilots were given orders based on the
assumption that Nagumo would continue on
his course toward Midway until his strike
planes were recovered at about 0900 hours.

Fletcher, in the *Yorktown*, had lost sight of
Task Force 16 soon after he had sent it dashing

on ahead; the two functioned almost as independent units through the rest of the battle. After he recovered his search planes he held back his own attack force for a time, waiting to see if any additional sighting reports would come in. When none did, he sent up his own planes at 0906 hours – 12 torpedo bombers, 17 dive bombers, and six Wildcats. Above his ship flew the Japanese scout plane, now joined by another float plane, the *Tone*, beaming a homing signal to be used later to guide a strike force directly to the carrier. From that moment the *Yorktown* was a marked ship.

Recovery operations had begun aboard the four Japanese carriers at 0837 hours, as they steamed toward Midway in a loose box formation – *Hiryu* and *Kaga* to the east, *Soryu* and *Akagi* to the west – inside a screen of two battleships, three cruisers, and 11 destroyers. But Nagumo was growing increasingly nervous as reconnaissance reports told him of a large force of carrier planes approaching; before his recovery was complete he turned east-northeast to contact the enemy carriers, while his crews worked hastily (and thus, somewhat carelessly) to rearm and refuel the planes.

Fortunately for the Japanese, this change in course caused 35 dive bombers and ten fighters from the *Hornet* to miss them completely; all of them eventually ran out of fuel and either made forced landings on Midway or ditched. The torpedo squadron from the *Hornet*, however, had ignored their orders and set off on their own course; at 0925 hours they spotted smoke from the Japanese ships and swooped down to attack in the face of heavy anti-aircraft fire and a large number of Zeros. Without air cover they had no chance – all 15 planes were shot down and 29 of the 30 pilots were killed. At 0930 the 14 torpedo bombers from the *Enterprise* arrived, also without fighter cover; ten were shot down and the remaining four were so badly battered they could hardly make their escape. At 1000 hours Torpedo 3 from the *Yorktown* arrived with six Wildcats, who were quickly driven off by about 15 Zeros in the only fighter plane action to take place over the Japanese fleet. Only five of the 12 torpedo planes and three of the Wildcats survived the attack. No hits had been registered by the 47 aircraft, only six of which returned.

Meanwhile, 37 dive bombers from the *Enterprise* had been searching vainly for the Japanese force when the leader of the Wildcat fighter squadron radioed that he was over the enemy fleet, but that he was short on fuel and was heading home. This was the first news that Spruance and Browning had had of their strike, and Lieutenant Commander Clarence McClusky, leader of the squadron, could hear Browning screaming, 'Attack! Attack!' over the radio. Replying 'Wilco, as soon as I find the bastards,' he headed toward the carriers. At 1002 hours the dive bombers raced down from 14,000 feet toward the *Akagi* and *Kaga*.

The Japanese ships had been forced to take violent evasive maneuvers to escape the torpedo attacks and had not been able to launch more defensive fighters, while those already in the air were at a low altitude and could not climb high enough to meet this new attack. The *Akagi*, with 40 planes refueling on deck, sustained three hits within two minutes; one of the bombs fell on a hangar containing stored torpedoes and another struck the fueling planes on the flight deck. At 1047 hours Nagumo reluctantly transferred his flag to the light cruiser, *Nagara*; by 1915 hours that evening the fiercely burning carrier had been abandoned. The *Kaga* took four hits; one killed everyone on the bridge, including the captain, while others started fires in the bomb and gasoline storage areas. She, too, was soon abandoned and sank at 1925 hours.

While the planes from the *Enterprise* were attacking *Akagi* and *Kaga*, 17 dive bombers from *Yorktown* were swooping down on the *Soryu*. Despite starting out nearly an hour and a half later than the other attack groups, they had arrived at the same time, thanks to smart navigating advice from Hubie Strange (the weatherman) and Oscar Pederson (the air group commander) aboard *Yorktown*. Attacking in three waves at one-minute intervals, they dropped three 1000lb bombs on *Soryu*'s flight deck. The ship burst into flames and had to be abandoned within twenty minutes. Damage control parties had the fires under control by 1145 hours, but then the submarine *Nautilus* re-entered the fray and put three torpedoes into the carrier, re-starting the fires. At 1610 hours the *Soryu* broke in half and slipped beneath the waves.

After the attacks the dive bombers headed back to their carriers. Most made it – some on literally their last gallon of gasoline – but a few had to ditch, owing to a miscalculation of the carriers' position. Three Japanese carriers had been left in flames, but the *Enterprise* had lost 14 of 37 dive bombers, ten of 14 torpedo bombers, and one Wildcat. The *Hornet* had lost all her torpedo bombers and 12 Wildcats, while her dive bombers had missed the battle entirely. *Yorktown* was down seven of 12 torpedo bombers, two dive bombers, and three Wildcats. Fletcher launched a search mission to find the fourth carrier; the *Hiryu* had been far ahead of the other three carriers, and had been missed by the first wave of American dive bombers.

Since he still had *Hiryu*, with a full complement of planes, Nagumo decided to carry on the battle, reasoning that the Americans had only one or two carriers which had already used most of their planes. He sent a message to Yamamoto: 'Sighted enemy composed of one carrier, five cruisers, and six destroyers at position bearing ten degrees 240 miles from Midway,' then he headed for the *Yorktown*.

The first Japanese attack group, composed of 18 Vals and six Zeros, was launched at 1100 hours, followed by a second group of ten Kates and six Zeros at 1331 hours. At the same time Admiral Kondo, who had intercepted the message to Yamamoto, signaled that he was coming north to support the carrier force, while Yamamoto ordered the light carriers *Ryujo* and *Junyo* south from the Aleutians to help.

By flying low, the Japanese planes managed to stay under the straight line beam of the *Yorktown*'s crude radar, and were not detected until they were only 46 miles from the ship. At noon the carrier began taking evasive action; the heavy cruisers *Astoria* and *Portland*, as well as the destroyers *Hammann*, *Anderson*, *Russell*, *Morris*, and *Hughes*, formed a defensive ring around her; the 12 Wildcats that were airborne as combat air patrol went out to intercept, joined by several Wildcats rushed over from *Hornet*. The first wave of 24 Japanese planes arrived at 1210 hours. In a dogfight to end all dogfights, the badly outnumbered interceptors knocked out ten Vals and three fighters, while anti-aircraft fire accounted for two more dive bombers. But three of the remaining six planes managed to score a hit. The first bomb damaged the boilers, the second started a fire that was put out by flooding, and

the third exploded on the flight deck, resulting in another fire and many casualties. Fletcher transferred his flag to the *Astoria*, since *Yorktown*'s communications equipment had been knocked out; but by 1340 hours repair parties had the carrier running at 18 knots again. The fighters were on deck refueling at 1630 hours when the second attack group was picked up on the radar. There were 12 Wildcats on combat air patrol, but the Kates and Zeros slipped by them and scored two torpedo hits which ruptured most of the fuel tanks on the port side, cut of all power, jammed the rudder, and caused a 17-degree list. Afraid that the *Yorktown* would capsize, and unable to repair the damage, Captain Elliott Buckmaster gave the order to abandon ship at 1500 hours.

'Old Yorky' stayed afloat, however, and on 6 June Fletcher sent a salvage party over on the destroyer *Hammann* to attempt to get her back to port. But the *Yorktown* had been sighted by a Japanese reconnaissance plane, and Submarine *I-168* commanded by one of Japan's great daredevil sailors, Commander Yahachi Tanabe, slipped through the destroyer screen. *I-168* put one torpedo into *Hammann*, which sank within four minutes, and two more into the *Yorktown* before escaping through a heavy depth charge attack to wind up what had been one of the greatest submarine exploits of the war. The *Yorktown* finally sank at 0500 hours on 7 June.

The *Hiryu* was finally spotted by one of the planes Fletcher had sent out just prior to the attack on the *Yorktown* and at 1630 hours 24 dive bombers from *Enterprise*, including ten refugees from the *Yorktown*, took off – without fighter cover, since all operational Wildcats were flying defensive formations. The group found the *Hiryu* at 1700 hours and scored four solid hits, losing only three of their number. B-17s from Midway made another attack about an hour later, but – with their usual bad luck – made no hits. Another group of five Vindicators and six dive bombers took off from Midway at 1900 hours, but could not locate the carrier. The *Hiryu* was abandoned by all hands except her captain at 0230 hours the next morning, and finally sank at 0900 hours.

For all intents and purposes, the Battle of Midway was over. Yamamoto, who had been several hundred miles northwest of Nagumo during the carrier battle of 4 June, considered

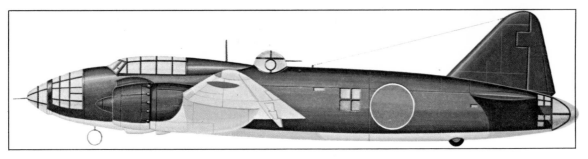

The Mitsubishi G4M2 Betty was an improved version of the G4M1, which was very vulnerable to enemy fire and easily burst into flames. The G4M1 took part in the Battle of Midway but was phased out shortly after and used for reconnaissance and suicide missions.

joining up with Kondo's Midway Occupation Force and the Aleutian force and engaging the Americans in a traditional naval battle. Nagumo, who disagreed, was summarily relieved of command. But as reports came in revealing that the Americans still had two operational carriers, while all four Japanese carriers were either sunk or abandoned, Yamamoto realized that a dawn air attack was more probable than a night gun battle. He therefore reluctantly ordered his forces to turn west.

Spruance, meanwhile, had quite rightly decided that a night engagement with a large Japanese force, far better equipped than he for night fighting, would not be to his advantage. He turned east and headed away from the battle area until midnight.

Midway was the first defeat ever suffered by the Japanese Navy, and news of the debacle was completely suppressed in Japan. All papers concerning the event were classified top secret and destroyed in 1945, so that the Japanese public only learned of the events at Midway in the 1950s when published accounts began to appear.

Japan lost four heavy carriers, one heavy cruiser, 322 planes, and 3500 men at Midway, against one heavy carrier, 150 planes, and 307 men for the Americans. Though Yamamoto blamed the disaster on the failure of his advance screen of submarines to locate and harass the Americans, in fact the responsibility for deploying the submarines in the wrong place was his. It was also Yamamoto who divided his huge fleet and then devised for it a rigid, highly complicated battle plan that was entirely based on what he assumed the Americans would do. The Americans did not follow the script, and the Japanese commanders were not trained to adapt rapidly to radically different situations.

But without the complete and accurate intelligence reports gathered by the Americans, the Japanese plan might well have succeeded. These reports, which gave Nimitz the time and the knowledge to correctly dispose his forces, were probably the crucial factor in the American victory.

The Battle of Midway is worthy of note in the history of naval warfare, in that it marks the end of the transition period between the eras dominated by battleships and by carriers. Even more than Coral Sea, Midway demonstrated the central role of the carrier plane. Despite a fleet that remained largely intact and immeasurably superior fire power, Yamamoto was forced to retire without firing a shot once he lost his air cover.

Midway saw the debut of the Zeke, or Zero-3 fighter plane. The original Zero had been far more maneuverable and had a rate of climb three times greater than its American counterparts, and the new Zero was a vast improvement. But the Japanese pilots proved to be inferior to the Americans, an indication of the deterioration of the Japanese air arm and the growing shortage of well-trained pilots since Pearl Harbor. On the American side, the Dauntless dive bomber, which was to become the most successful carrier plane of the war, performed superbly, while the Devastator torpedo bomber proved so disappointing that it was taken off the list of naval combat planes and replaced by the new Avenger.

The Battle of Midway did not decide the entire course of the Pacific War in a moment, nor did it end with the utter destruction of one of the combatants. Its importance lies in the fact that it broke Japan's naval superiority and restored the balance between the two navies. Once that had happened, as Yamamoto foresaw, it was only a matter of time until economic mobilization allowed America to overwhelm Japan.

This TBF Avenger was the
sole survivor of its squadron
after the Battle of Midway.

JAP LOSES PANTS TRYING TO SAVE FACE
MIDWAY ISLANDS, JUNE 4th 1942

TO:
ADMIRAL NIMITZ (CINCPAC)
COMPLIMENTS OF:
MARINE DEFENSE FORCE
COLONEL, USMC, COMMANDING

This cartoon was drawn by an artist of the 6th Marine Defense battalion shortly after Midway. The original was presented to Admiral Nimitz by Colonel Harold Shannon, commanding officer of the unit.

Florida I

TULAGI GAVUTU

0740/1200,
2 Marine Regt plus 1 Para Bn
Strong resistance overcome

Savo I

**7 August 1942
US 1 Marine Div**
(Vandegrift)

I R O N B O T T O M   S O U N D

1/7 Feb 1943,
Japanese forces
withdraw

C
Esperance

TENARO

**October,
Japanese reserves
land**

*Tassafaronga
Pt*

17 Jan 1943,
Jap Seventeenth Army
begins withdrawal from
the Matanikau

PM, 8 Aug
Henderson Field
taken

0909,
5 Marine Regt lands
unopposed
1 Marine Regt follows

Night 7/8 Sept
Marine raiders
attack Jap base

Koli Pt

Aug
Sept

TAIVU

Lunga Pt

KUKUM

TENARU

23/26 Oct,
Maruyama's attacks
repulsed

**Night 20/21 Aug,
Ichiki's detachment
destroyed**

Matanikau   *Mt Austen*

Bloody Ridge

Lunga   *Tenaru*

12/14 Sept,
Kawaguchi suffers
heavy losses at
Bloody Ridge

G u a d a l c a n a l

AMERICAN ATTACKS

JAPANESE COUNTERATTACKS
AND WITHDRAWALS

US DEFENSE PERIMETER 9 AUGUST

US POSITIONS 23 OCTOBER

EARLY DECEMBER, 1 MARINE DIV RELIEVED BY 25 INF, 2 MARINE AND AMERICAL DIVS (XIV CORPS [PATCH])

0   MILES   10
0   KILOMETERS   20

4 GUADALCANAL
The Jungle Nightmare

Following the US victory at Guadalcanal, the island was used as a staging post for the advance through the Solomons.

Immediately after the Battle of Midway, the central point of the war in the Pacific moved back to the Southwest Pacific Area again. The Japanese wished to strengthen their hold in that area, and decided to temporarily give up the plan to disrupt communications between the Australians and Americans. Japanese planners decided on a two-fold maneuver, beginning with an overland campaign from the north coast of New Guinea to capture the vital supply base at Port Moresby, and at the same time consolidating their position in the Solomons.

Meanwhile, American interest in the southern Solomons was picking up considerably. The two overall commanders were Admiral Chester Nimitz and General Douglas Mac-Arthur, men who were not used to being on the defensive. The pressure was now off Hawaii for the moment and the time was ripe for a limited offensive against the Japanese. The important question was where to strike and who would command the offensive. This was settled by a Joint Chiefs of Staff directive on 2 July 1942, ordering a parallel advance

Right: Vice-Admiral John McCain and Major General Alexander Vandegrift on an American base in the Solomons in 1942.

Below: Rear Admiral Richmond Kelly Turner and Major General Alexander Vandegrift on board the USS *McCawley*.

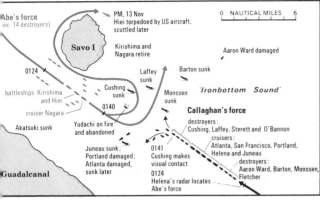

Abe's force (inc 14 destroyers)

Savo I

PM, 13 Nov
Hiei torpedoed by US aircraft,
scuttled later

0 NAUTICAL MILES 6

Kirishima and Nagara retire

Aaron Ward damaged

0124

battleships Kirishima and Hiei

Laffey sunk
Barton sunk

Cushing sunk

Monssen sunk

'Ironbottom Sound'

cruiser Nagara

0140

Callaghan's force

Akatsuki sunk

Yudachi on fire and abandoned

destroyers:
Cushing, Laffey, Sterett and O'Bannon
cruisers:
Atlanta, San Francisco, Portland,
Helena and Juneau

Juneau sunk;
Portland damaged;
Atlanta damaged,
sunk later

0141
Cushing makes
visual contact

destroyers:
Aaron Ward, Barton, Monssen,
Fletcher

Guadalcanal

0124
Helena's radar locates
Abe's force

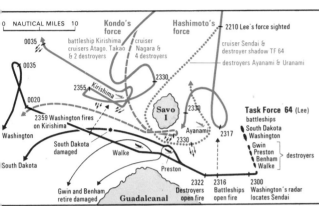

0 NAUTICAL MILES 10

Kondo's force
battleship Kirishima
cruisers Atago, Takao
& 2 destroyers

Hashimoto's force
cruiser Nagara &
4 destroyers

2210 Lee's force sighted

cruiser Sendai &
destroyer shadow TF 64

destroyers Ayanami & Uranami

0035

0035

0020

2355 Kirishima

2330

2359 Washington fires
on Kirishima

Washington

South Dakota
damaged

Savo I

2330

Ayanami

2330

2317

Task Force 64 (Lee)
battleships
South Dakota
Washington

Gwin
Preston
Benham
Walke } destroyers

South Dakota

Walke

Preston

Gwin and Benham
retire damaged

2322
Destroyers
open fire

2316
Battleships
open fire

2300
Washington's radar
locates Sendai

Guadalcanal

upon Rabaul, up the Solomons and along the New Guinea coast. It was to be accomplished in three stages: the seizure of the Santa Cruz Islands, then Tulagi and the adjacent islands; the occupation of the Solomons, with Papua and New Guinea up to the Huon Peninsula; finally, the capture of Rabaul and the remainder of the Bismarck Archipelago. The initial phase of this operation was code named Watchtower. Also the boundary between the Southwest Pacific and Pacific Ocean Commands was moved slightly so that some of the Solomons came under Nimitz's sphere of operational control. MacArthur was to oversee the completion of the final two phases.

On 5 July 1942 reconnaissance aircraft confirmed the reports of the Australian coastwatchers that the Japanese had transferred large troop concentrations from Tulage to the nearby island of Guadalcanal, and were building an airfield of unknown proportions. This news threw a monkeywrench into the entire operation, if the Japanese were allowed to complete an airfield unopposed, they would

be able to launch fighters and bombers at all Allied attempts to move into the Solomons and the Coral Sea. The all-important objective was now to seize Guadalcanal and the strategic air-strip at Lunga Point, later to be renamed Henderson Field, and consequently the Santa Cruz portion was dropped from the agenda.

Guadalcanal was no paradise as the Marines who fought and died there knew well. It was a hell hole, an island forgotten in time. Ninety miles long and 25 miles wide, a mixture of rain forests, stinking malarial swamps, thick grass-lands and undergrowth, and steep, treacherous mountains; that was Guadalcanal, a strategic objective for a few months on a general's map which later as the war progressed would be forgotten and returned to its semi-primeval state of existence. The 'Canal' as it became known to the Marines who fought on it and to the American people who read about it in their daily papers, was situated in the southern half of the Solomons group, which comprises many islands running for 600 miles in a southeast direction from Rabaul, Buka and Bougainville. The remaining islands and atolls form a double chain separated by a deep channel which was given the name of the 'Slot.'

In the weeks which followed, plans were thrashed out, differences settled, troops gather-ed and an overall strategic commander selected, Vice-Admiral Robert Ghormley. The am-phibious force was commanded by Rear Admiral Richmond Kelly Turner. Rear Admiral Frank Fletcher, who commanded the carrier task force at the Battles of the Coral Sea and Midway, was in command of the carriers off Guadalcanal and provided air cover for the operation. The air support force was composed of the carriers *Enterprise*, *Saratoga* and *Wasp* screened by the new battleship *North Carolina*, six cruisers and 16 destroyers. The convoy of transports consisted of four cruisers and 11 destroyers, and was to carry the 1st US Marine Division. The Marine force was commanded by a crusty old fighter, Major General Alex-ander Archer Vandegrift. The convoy was screened by Rear Admiral Victor Crutchley with a force of three Australian and two American cruisers (HMS *Australia*, *Canberra* and *Hobart*, USS *Chicago* and USS *San Juan*).

The operation was being supported by land-based aircraft from airfields in Fiji, New Caledonia and the New Hebrides, and also from

army aircraft under MacArthur's command. There were to be two landings, the first on the larger island of Guadalcanal and the second on the much smaller island of Tulagi.

Although these preparations seemed quite thorough, in fact, the organization behind the operation left much to be desired. Vandegrift had been given very little time to train his men and get them acclimatized. Although the 1st Marine Division had a core of seasoned veterans, most of the men were new recruits with no fighting experience. The Operation was nicknamed Operation Shoestring because it had been so hastily put together. Vandegrift pushed the target date back by a week for a landing on 7 August but could not get a further extension. Thus much equipment and materiel was left on the docks at Wellington, New Zealand. The amphibious force set off on 22nd July and met the air support task force south of Fiji; after a four-day practice on a remote island of the group, they set sail for the 'Canal' on 31 July. The force was undetected in its approach because of heavy haze and inter-mittent rain squalls. On 7 August the initial landings were made on Red Beach at Guadalcanal near Lunga Point and on Tulagi. There was no opposition on Guadalcanal as all the Japanese technicians had fled into the jungle and by nightfall 11,000 Marines were ashore. On the next day, the airfield was secured and the Marines put out scouts to ascertain what the Japanese were planning. On Tulagi the situation was not as clear-cut, the Japanese were better prepared, and the three battalions of Marines met stiff resistance. By 8 August Tulagi was completely under Marine control, the casualties were 108 Marines dead and 140 wounded. The Japanese garrison of 1500 troops was practically exterminated to a man. Meanwhile, it had taken only 48 hours to gain the initial foothold on the 'Canal,' but it would be another six months of intense and bitter fighting before it could be secured. The scene was now set for one of the cruellest, hardest fought campaigns in the Pacific.

Japanese actions were swift: immediately after the US landings, a striking force from the 25th Air Flotilla was dispatched from Rabaul. On 7 and 8 August, Japanese bombers attacked the transports lying off Lunga Point and would have caused heavy damage, except for the timely warnings given by the Australian coastwatchers. The attacks were intercepted by US aircraft from the naval carriers but two destroyers were hit and one transport was lost. The Marines were digging in around Henderson Field and prepared for a major Japanese attack.

Left: A Marine landing craft hits the beach with a thud. The purpose of landing in a jungle area was to afford the men immediate protection in the undergrowth.

Below left: Marines patrol the jungle trying to extend their control on the island.

Bottom left: Another landing operation, this time on a beach. Guadalcanal was the place where the US Army and Marines perfected their landing techniques which would hold them in good stead throughout the war in the Pacific.

When the news of the landings reached Rabaul, Admiral Gunichi Mikawa was in the middle of preparing for a major offensive against Port Moresby. He immediately guessed American intentions and decided to send all available ships to attack and destroy the US naval forces off Guadalcanal, and then to reinforce and exterminate the Marine landing force on the island. By 7 August, five heavy and two light cruisers were sailing toward the 'Canal.' To make matters worse, Imperial General Headquarters issued orders to reinforce the garrison of the island and a convoy carrying 500 additional troops, with a destroyer escort were *en route*. But shortly after setting sail one of the transports was torpedoed by an American submarine, so the convoy was recalled to Rabaul.

On the beach itself, the supply and logistics problems were mounting for Vandegrift, who was trying to keep to his original timetable. At 1400 hours, he ordered the 1st Battalion, 5th Marines to advance westward to Alligator Creek and dig in for the night. By 1600 hours Vandegrift was ashore and had established his forward command post. During all this the Japanese were far from idle, they had launched two air strikes. The first was at 1320 hours and consisted of 24 aircraft of the Japanese 25th Air Flotilla. Warning was received from an Australian coastwatcher and a welcoming party was arranged. Twelve Japanese aircraft were shot down by Wildcats from the *Saratoga*, but the USS *Mugford,* a destroyer, was hit and 22 men killed. Two hours later there was an attack by ten Aichi E16A1 dive bombers but no serious damage was recorded. The First Marine Combat Group 'B,' commanded by Colonel Clifton Cates had been ordered by Vandegrift to proceed to Mount Austen but they were held up due to the terrific heat and tropical undergrowth. Vandegrift realized that Mount Austen would not be reached that day; so he changed his plans accordingly. The Marines were to secure their positions and dig in for the night. The next morning the Marines would push forward toward the Lunga and bypass Mount Austen, occupying the airstrip from the south. The 5th Marines were to advance on Lunga also and then continue to Kukum. There were many shaky Marines on the first night but the Japanese did not make the expected counterattack. On Saturday, 8

August, the 1st Battalion, 5th Marines, supported by the 1st Tank Battalion, succeeded in crossing the mouth of Alligator Creek. The Marines believed that this was in fact the Tenaru River, but it was in reality the Ilu. The 1st Battalion, 1st Marines, acting on orders swung west away from Mount Austen and began to advance. This unit moved very slowly and had difficulty crossing one of the numerous creeks in its path. The other units, the 2nd and 3rd Battalions made faster progress through the jungle than their counterparts in the 1st. The day was extremely hot and humid to say the least and by the end of the day the 1st Battalion had passed the airfield, but the 2nd and 3rd Battalions had in their turn slowed down and were still south of the airfield when the order came to dig in for the night.

The 5th Marines made good progress and managed to take a few Japanese prisoners. It was gathered from information sweated out of the enemy that no Japanese resistance would be encountered within the next 48 hours. Vandegrift took immediate advantage of this situation and ordered the 5th Marines to advance more rapidly. The regiment crossed the Lunga over the main bridge, and by skirting the airfield to the north, it took Kukum along with large quantities of supplies.

Meanwhile the situation on the beach was not going according to plan and after another attack by Japanese Betty bombers escorted by Zero fighters, Fletcher's fighter strength was being gradually thinned down. From 99 aircraft, he was now down to 78 and was also dangerously low on fuel reserves. Fletcher decided that he was putting his entire Task Force 61 in jeopardy if he remained off Guadalcanal any longer and asked Ghormley for permission to withdraw his carriers. Ghormley was not too happy with this request but because he was too far removed from the scene felt that it would be unreasonable to deny such an urgent request. This decision was the most controversial made during the entire Guadalcanal campaign. The main points being that only 50 percent of the supplies for the Marine force had been unloaded; Fletcher still had enough fuel for at least 72 hours and the Japanese air attacks had been beaten off; and the majority of ships were undamaged. However Mikawa's force was steaming down the 'Slot' making for Guadalcanal. US aircraft had sighted the Japanese

Left: Marines search a pine grove on Guadalcanal, trying to flush out snipers.

Below left: Marines dig in around Henderson Field. Fighting was concentrated around the air strip for the first three months of the campaign.

Bottom left: The bodies left following the Battle of Bloody Ridge on 13-14 September 1942.

squadron on the evening of 7 August but due to a belated report, giving the wrong information and bad weather, the enemy was not located again that day. Therefore, Mikawa was able to make his approach down the 'Slot' undetected.

Turner summoned Rear Admiral Crutchley and Major General Vandegrift aboard his flagship the USS *McCawley*, and relayed the in-

formation to them that Fletcher was pulling out and taking their air cover and supplies with him. Vandegrift's response to this was not recorded, but he must have been very angry. While Turner was expanding on the details, Mikawa's force sailed right past the picket destroyers and turned their guns to bear point blank at the unsuspecting *Canberra* and *Chicago*. The *Canberra* was hit so hard that she had to be

Far left: Faced by mounting casualties and the impossibility of reinforcing and resupplying his men, General Hyakutake had to admit defeat. In December, when these pictures were taken, the Japanese began secretly to evacuate those men who had survived the Guadalcanal campaign.

Left: A machine-gun emplacement on Guadalcanal.

abandoned but the *Chicago* was more fortunate, and received no crippling damage. The Japanese did not wait to see the result of their surprise attack but sailed out of range and toward the northern patrol group. The southern patrol group was so confused that no warning was sent to the northern group. The northern group fared worse than its Southern counterparts. The Japanese sunk the USS *Astoria*, *Vincennes* and *Quincy* in less than an hour. Mikawa had taken the US Navy by surprise and the result was an astounding victory which would have been even more resounding if he had taken the initiative and destroyed the unprotected transports. It is only conjecture but the entire campaign on the 'Canal' would have changed, and possibly the war in the Pacific taken a different turn if the transports

had been eliminated.

This disaster, and disaster is exactly what it was, confirmed Fletcher's belief that he must remove his task force from the danger zone. The 9 August was spent in preparation for departure and by sunset Task Force 61 was steaming away. The Marines under Vandegrift were now completely on their own. The situation was not very inviting. The US Navy had lost control of the seas in the Solomons. The nearest air support was in Espiritu Santo in the New Hebrides. Supplies were already beginning to run out, and morale was not very high after what most Marines thought was naval desertion. Vandegrift realized that he was in no position to attack, so his schedule stressed defense. His most important operational concern was to make the airstrip functional at all costs. An extended perimeter defense was established around the airfield. The Marines set up .30 and .50 caliber machine-guns, backed up by 37mm guns and 90mm AA guns all around the defensive perimeter. The feeling of being abandoned was considerably lessened on 14 August when the Navy ran the gauntlet of enemy aircraft and surface ships to bring supplies of ammunition and fuel, as well as the bare essentials to the Marines at Guadalcanal. Vandegrift decided to make a small foray against the Japanese by driving them across the Matanikau. This action was successful but did not allay the doubts in his mind of the ability of his men to sustain and repulse a heavy attack from the numerically superior Japanese force on the island. The major thing which aided the Marines was the Japanese confusion over exactly what to do – the Japanese believed that the US would eventually get tired of the 'insignificant' island and withdraw. Japanese intelligence showed that the Marines were digging in and this put a whole new picture on the screen. Plans were made to expel the Marines from Guadalcanal. Lieutenant General Haruyoshi Hyakutake, 17th Army Commander was ordered to retake Tulagi and Guadalcanal before setting out on the all important mission of securing Port Moresby. Hyakutake had over 50,000 men in his 17th Army but he had a slight problem, they were spread out all over the Pacific. Undaunted, he believed that if he could send one really crack unit into the islands that the Marine force

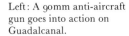

Left: A 90mm anti-aircraft gun goes into action on Guadalcanal.

could be driven into the sea and utterly destroyed. He chose Colonel Kiyanao Ichiki's 28th Infantry from Guam to accomplish the task. At the time, he appeared to be the ideal man for the task at hand but events proved him to be impetuous and rash. On 18 August he was to take 900 men on six destroyers and land at Taivu Point, around 20 miles from the Marine positions. The remainder of his 2500 men outfit would join him within the week.

Vandegrift was being kept up to date by his native coastwatchers and knew that Japanese forces were building up in the east. Captain Charles Brush set out on a patrol on 19 August with Marines of Abel Company, 1st Marines and headed toward Koli Point. At noon Japanese troops were sighted, Brush sent his executive officer, Lieutenant Joseph Jachym round to flank them and put them in a crossfire between the two marine columns. The result was 31 out of 35 Japanese dead. From

the documents and maps taken from the bodies it was discovered that they were army personnel and not navy men who had previously been fighting the Marines on Guadalcanal.

Ichiki attacked the Marine positions on the mouth of Alligator Creek on the Ilu River (still called the Tenaru by the US), early on 21 August. He recklessly decided that the 900 men he had brought with him would be sufficient and he need not wait for the rest of his 2500 man force. The Japanese made two attempts: the first at 0240 hours and the second at 0500 hours, both attacks were repulsed with heavy casualties to the attackers. Some of the Japanese were caught on the far bank of the river and Colonel Gerald Thomas, Divisional Operations Officer, recommended to Vandegrift to counterattack immediately and drive the survivors into the sea. Vandegrift ordered the reserve battalion, Cate's 1st Battalion, 1st Marines under Lieutenant Colonel Creswell

to cross the river and drive all Japanese troops downstream. Meanwhile Pollock's men provided a heavy and continuous fire from the other side of the river. Also to insure total success a platoon of light tanks were brought up and Marine aircraft would be utilized to strafe the entire affected area. Needless to say, the operation was a complete success. In Vandegrift's own words 'the rear of the tanks looked like meat grinders.' By 1700 hours the Battle of Tenaru (Ilu) was finished. The Marines had killed over 800 Japanese, taken 15 prisoners and of the survivors, most of these died in the jungle. Colonel Ichiki survived the battle but upon reaching Taivu, he shot himself after burning his regimental colors.

The Battle of Tenaru was an American victory but there was still a great deal to be done before Vandegrift's position on Guadalcanal could be called secure. The Japanese became even more determined than ever to drive the

Marines off the island. To make the airfield serviceable, US Marine Corps engineers utilized captured Japanese equipment, as their own was still on board the transports. On 12 August the aide to Rear Admiral John McCain flew a Catalina flying boat onto the airfield for an inspection of the runway. McCain was responsible for land-based air operations. The strip was only 2600ft long, with no drainage and no steel matting coverage, and finally there were no taxiways. The aide was a realistic man and passed the field as fit for fighter aircraft operations. The airfield was named Henderson Field after a hero of the Battle of Midway. The first aircraft arrived on 20 August; 12 Dauntless dive bombers commanded by Major Richard Mangrum and 19 Marine Wildcat fighters under Captain John Smith.

The Japanese had gathered two task forces consisting of three aircraft carriers, eight

Below: On board the USS *San Juan* during the Battle of Santa Cruz in October 1942. On the horizon is heavy anti-aircraft fire, indicating the USS *Hornet* under attack.

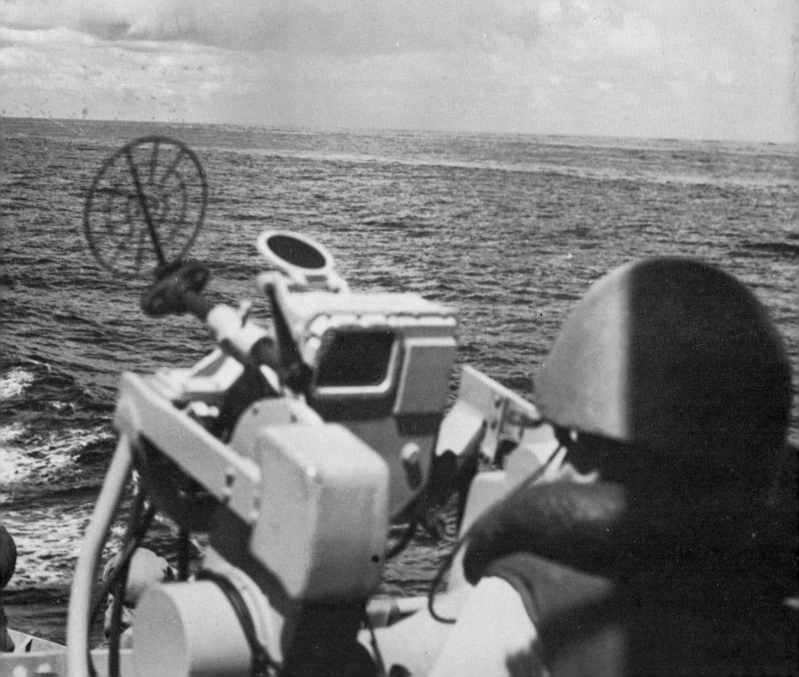

battleships, four heavy cruisers, two light cruisers, 21 destroyers and other vessels, with air cover provided by the 25th Air Flotilla at Rabaul. To meet this small armada, Fletcher had at his disposal three aircraft carriers, one battleship, four cruisers and destroyers. The resulting battle became known as the Battle of the Eastern Solomons and was very like Midway, except that the result was a stalemate. Dogfights were now a matter of daily routine for the Marines. But without these pilots and the support crews of the 'Cactus Air Force' as it became known, Vandegrift's Marines might not have held their beach-head in the black days of August and September 1942. These Marine pilots lived in tents and dug-outs, their staple diet was rice and spam but they were the actual front line of resistance at the 'Canal.' Still at the beginning of September, Vandegrift's position was not very reassuring to say the least. His battle-weary troops were hungry, stricken with dysentery and jungle rot and by October malaria would also take its toll. The Marines could not get an uninterrupted night's sleep because of the Japanese night prowler aircraft nicknamed 'Louie the Louse' and 'Washing Machine Charlie.' Morale in the American camp was falling. Tension mounted as the Americans had to wait for the Japanese to act.

Admiral Raizo Tanaka managed time after time to run the gauntlet with night-time runs to reinforce Guadalcanal. This became so regular that the Marines called it the 'Tokyo Express.' Vandegrift was in desperate need of reinforcements with the Japanese landing more and more troops to both the east and west of his perimeter. He transferred troops from Tulagi to Guadalcanal, including the experienced Edson's Raiders. The Marines kept making occasional thrusts into the Japanese held areas to keep the enemy on their toes and to gather intelligence information. On

10 September, one of Vandegrift's urgent requests was granted; down to only 11 out of the original 38 Wildcats, Ghormley sent an immediate 24 replacements. Colonel Edson moved his command post and his mixed force of Raiders and Parachutists to a ridge one mile south of Henderson Field and not far from Vandegrift's own headquarters. This ridge was 1000 yards long, running northwest to southeast, and surrounded by steep undulating thick jungle growth. This was to be renamed Bloody Ridge in a few days.

Edson deployed his 700 men in the prime locations for a possible Japanese penetration attempt. The Jungle was cleared out and barbed wire strung out between the trees to give it the appearance of a perimeter. In direct support of Edson's men were 105mm howitzers and the 2nd Marine Battalion, 5th Marines. On 12 September the long-awaited Japanese attack was at last launched. It started off with an intense naval bombardment of the Marine positions, followed up immediately by heavy mortar and artillery and then an all-out infantry attack by Kawaguchi's troops. The Marines were displaced from their positions but through faulty communications and the disorientation of their men, the Japanese attack lost impetus and stopped. The Marines under Edson then charged and retook their former positions along the ridge. Now started the long process of redigging in, laying more barbed wire and getting ready for the next attack which would surely come. The noise was intense, again naval bombardment, artillery and mortar barrages and the follow up infantry but Kawaguchi threw 2000 men

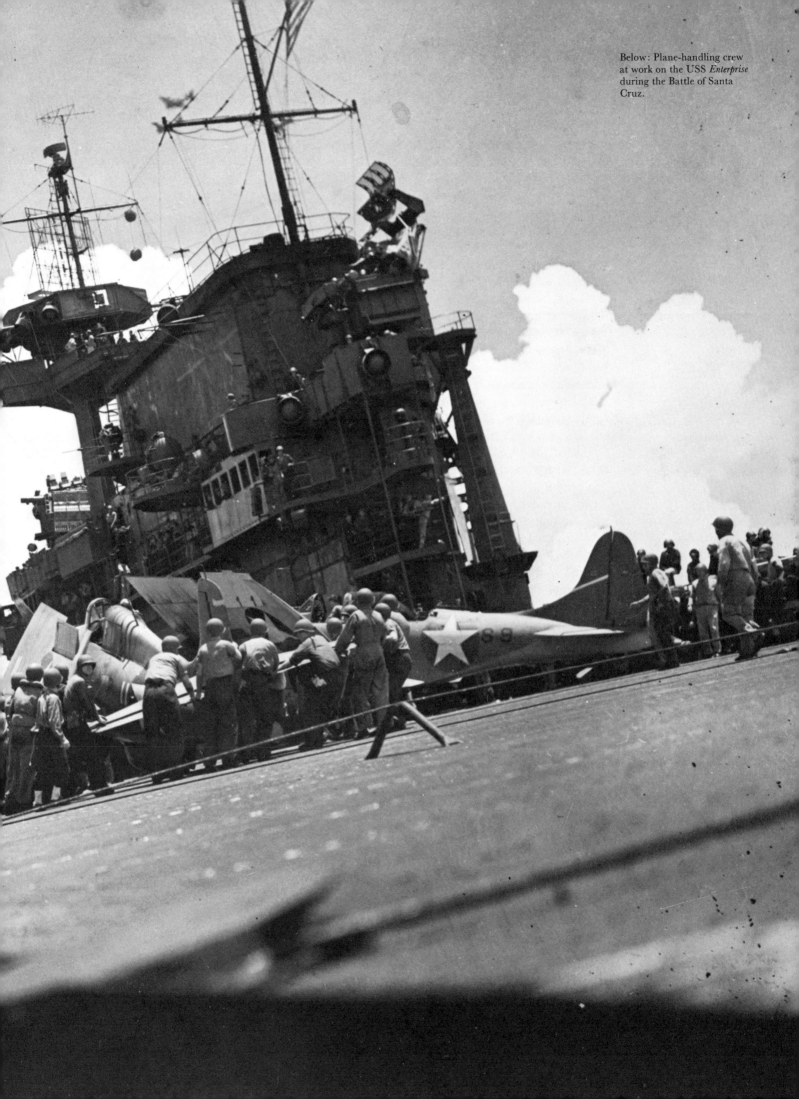

Below: Plane-handling crew at work on the USS *Enterprise* during the Battle of Santa Cruz.

Vice-Admiral William Halsey was made Commander in Chief of Southeast Pacific Fleet in October 1942. His brief was to sort out a difficult situation, which he managed to resolve successfully by December.

across the slope on 13 September. This mass wave of men was something which the Marines had never experienced before, as fast as they cut them down, their comrades just climbed over their dead bodies. The Marines were at the breaking point when 'Red Mike' Edson took the front himself and urged his weary men to smoke down all the enemy. Edson called for increased artillery support and practically brought it down to his own positions. Another stalwart was Major Kenneth Bailey who kept screaming at the top of his lungs the traditional Marine Corps cry 'Do you want to live forever.' Between the intense and accurate fire coming from the Marines on the ridge and the perfect artillery support, the Japanese were being decimated. By 14 September the Japanese were defeated and Kawaguchi knew it. The remainder of his force were retreating to Matanikau. The result of Bloody Ridge was an ocean of dead and wounded. Japanese dead totaled over 700 with an additional 600 wounded. The US casualties were 59 dead and 204 wounded. The US Marines had won another total victory but this was to be over-shadowed again by a defeat at sea.

Admiral Turner was keeping his word and was rushing reinforcements to Guadalcanal. This was the 7th Marines which he had picked up at the New Hebrides after their stint of duty on Samoa. The task force and its carrier escort force was sighted on 14 September by a Japanese aircraft. Turner remained on course until nightfall and then withdrew *McCawley* and the six precious transports and its cargo of 4000 Marines. The carriers *Hornet* and *Wasp*, the battleship *North Carolina* and various escort destroyers continued on course. On 15 September, at 0220 hours, the Japanese submarines *I-15* and *I-19* attacked the carrier force. The result of this attack was devastating: the *Wasp* was abandoned and sunk by the *Lansdowne*, the *North Carolina* had a 30 by 18ft gaping hole put in its side below the waterline and the destroyer *O'Brien* was also sunk. This naval action was off the Santa Cruz islands and again the US Navy had suffered another blow by the Imperial Navy. Turner's decision to withdraw was vindicated by his safe arrival at Guadalcanal and the landing of the 4000 men and some supplies. There was a brief lull in the fighting while both sides experimented and probed with the enemy's defensive posi-

tions. The Marines lost a few skirmishes and won a few but it was not until November that the offensive really got under way. The US was determined not to lose its hold on Guadalcanal. But as the struggle reached its climax, President Roosevelt ordered the Chiefs of Staff to send all available equipment, supplies and troops to the two priority theaters – the Pacific and North Africa – even if this meant drastically reducing strategic commitments elsewhere. Admiral King, CNO, could not send any carriers to the South Pacific, but he diverted a sizeable force to SOPAC, including a battleship, six cruisers, 24 submarines and 130 naval aircraft. General George Marshall, Army Chief of Staff, also sent an additional 75 army aircraft from Hawaii to reinforce the southwest Pacific but would not increase the troop commitment to the area, especially with the pressure on from Operation Torch, the Allied landings in North Africa. However, reinforcements were stripped from the other island bases and sent to the 'Canal.' On 4 November two regiments from the 2nd Marine Division were landed and a further 6000 officers and men were landed on 6 November from Noumea and Espiritu Santo (the latter were troops of the American Division). The two convoys were commanded by Rear Admiral Turner, and were escorted by two squadrons, the first under Rear Admiral Nicholas Scott and the second under Rear Admiral Daniel Callaghan. This force was shadowed by a task force formed around the hastily refitted *Enterprise* and the two battleships *Washington* and *South Dakota*. The Japanese were still no less determined than the US Marines to gain complete control over Guadalcanal, and November saw another major attempt to reinforce the island and force the Marines out once and for all. Their plan was basically no different from all previous attempts. Bombardment by two naval squadrons of Henderson Field, followed up again by artillery and mortar fire and a massive infantry break-through. The only difference this time was that a 3rd squadron was escorting the rest of the 38th Division from Rabaul, while a 4th squadron gave support. This was by far the largest planned general offensive to date.

Unknowingly, the US convoy, escorted by Rear Admiral Scott's squadron arrived off Lunga Point early on 11 November and was joined by Callaghan's squadron on 12 November. Just a few hours later, a strong Japanese naval force, including the battleships *Hiei* and *Kirishima*, was sighted steaming down the 'Slot.' Turner, nonplussed, calmly finished unloading the transports of all troops and supplies and then sailed in convoy for Espiritu Santo, only escorted by three destroyers. The remainder of the combined escort forces commanded by Rear Admiral Callaghan stayed behind to engage the enemy fleet, although outnumbered by superior Japanese forces, he did so to cover Turner's withdrawal.

After escorting the transports clear of the anchorage, Callaghan steered west to engage the enemy. It was an extremely dark and dismal night with no moon. In the early hours of the morning of 13 November, both forces practically collided before opening fire. The battle which followed lasted only 24 minutes and must go on record for being one of the most furious sea engagments ever fought. The Japanese lost two destroyers. The battleship *Hiei* was critically damaged, and left dead in the water for the US aircraft to finish off the next day. The US task force lost two light cruisers and four destroyers; both Rear Admirals Callaghan and Scott were killed in the battle and casualties were heavy. Callaghan's action accomplished his main objective allowing the task force time to intervene. The following afternoon, naval aircraft from the carrier *Enterprise* sank a cruiser and severely damaged other surface ships of the Japanese cruiser bombardment force. Furthermore, aircraft from Henderson Field inflicted grave damage to the transports unloading on the north side of the island and sunk seven out of 11. The Japanese heavy bombardment force was now reorganized and reinforced to cover the transports. It was composed of the battleship *Kirishima*, four cruisers and nine destroyers. Vice-Admiral 'Bull' Halsey, who had relieved Ghormley on 18 October, sent Rear Admiral Willis Lee with the battleships *Washington* and *South Dakota*, and four destroyers to attack it. Lee led his small squadron around the southeast tip of Guadalcanal and just after midnight engaged the enemy in the narrow channel south of Savo Island. This battle was fought at a longer range than the preceeding one, but the fighting was just as intense. The *Kirishima* was so heavily damaged

that she had to be scuttled; and one Japanese and three US destroyers had been sunk. The *South Dakota* was damaged but remained afloat. At daylight on 15 November, the four remaining Japanese transports were spotted by the Marines aground and helpless; shore batteries opened up and aided by aircraft from Henderson Field turned them into blazing hulks. Out of 10,000 troops which sailed with the ill-fated expedition, only 4000 arrived and they were without equipment or rations. The three-day battle of Guadalcanal was the first decisive victory for the US Navy since the beginning of the Solomons campaign.

At the end of November the Japanese tried once more to reinforce Guadalcanal, but Halsey sent out a squadron of five cruisers and four destroyers to intercept it. On 30 November, this cruiser squadron encountered eight Japanese destroyers attempting to bring supplies and reinforcements to the garrison at Tassafaronga. Only one Japanese destroyer was sunk, but the US Navy had four of its cruisers hit by torpedoes. This was the last of the midnight encounters in the narrow waters of the South Solomons. On the last day of 1942 Japanese Imperial General Headquarters decided to abandon Guadalcanal and fall back to a line of defense based on New Georgia. On 9 December General Alexander Patch relieved Vandegrift and during the next two months the 1st Marine Division was withdrawn for a much needed rest to Australia. It was relieved by the 25th US Division on 31 December. On 4 January 1943 the 2nd Marine Division Headquarters and 6th Marine Regiment arrived from New Zealand, bringing the strength of the Guadalcanal garrison to 50,000 men. The Japanese on the other hand were down to 25,000 effectives. They were underfed and disease-ridden, but were still willing to fight to the last man. General Imamura, Commander in Chief, 8th Area Army ordered them to Cape Esperance, from where they were to be evacuated during the first week in February. Exactly six months after the first US Marines landed at Red Beach on Guadalcanal, the last Japanese had been safely evacuated from the 'Canal.' General Patch was left in undisputed control of the island. This was the first US land victory achieved in World War II and marked the limits of Japanese territorial expansion.

The five Sullivan brothers served on the USS *Juneau*. The *Juneau* was sunk during the Naval Battle of Guadalcanal and all five brothers lost their lives.

The battleship *Iowa* bombards
Tinian during June 1944.

5 PHILIPPINE SEA
The Great Marianas Turkey Shoot

Right: Vice-Admiral Jisaburo Ozawa, commander of the Japanese carrier fleet.

Far right: Admiral Mineichi Koga, who drew up the plans for the A-Go operation in the Philippine Sea, died before he could witness its disastrous consequences.

The Great Marianas Turkey Shoot

In 1943 the Japanese tide of conquest in the Far East was stemmed and American forces began to erode Japan's outer defense perimeter. The Gilbert Islands were secured by the US in late November 1943, and in January 1944 an assault upon the Marshall Islands was equally successful. The Japanese found it impossible to react. The Combined Fleet, based at Truk, was merely a shadow of its former self, with the carriers still in Japan training replacement air groups and the cruiser force, attacked by the Americans at Rabaul, virtually a nonentity. It became even less effective in mid-February when Task Force 58 attacked Truk itself, forcing a withdrawal to Palau. As this threatened the flank of MacArthur's advance in New Guinea, however, Palau was also attacked in late March and Combined Fleet headquarters under Admiral Mineichi Koga, who had replaced Yamamoto when the latter was killed in June 1943, was removed to Mindanao. Unfortunately Koga was killed in the process when his seaplane crashed in bad weather, and he was replaced by Admiral Soemu Toyoda who decided to set up his headquarters in Japan, delegating the sea-going command known as the First Mobile Fleet, to Vice-Admiral Jisaburo Ozawa. It was to be a fatal split, denying initiative to the commander on the spot and subjecting the Japanese navy to the

false hopes and political machinations of Tokyo.

The results were apparent in the intricate plan put forward by Toyoda (Operation A-Go), designed to bring about 'a decisive battle with full strength . . . at a favorable opportunity.' The idea was to lure the American fleet into one of two battle areas (Palau or the Caroline Islands), chosen because they were within range of the myriad of island air bases from which Japanese air strength could participate to help balance the American carriers. A portion of the Japanese fleet was to be used as bait, sailing openly into the chosen area, and as soon as the Americans reacted the main portion under Ozawa was to leave its anchorage at Tawi Tawi in the Sulu Archipelago, proceed to an area east of the Philippines and take the enemy by surprise. It was an optimistic scenario, but once the Americans threatened the Mariana Islands, the next logical step after the Marshalls, the Japanese had to do something. The Marianas, consisting principally of the islands of Guam, Saipan and Tinian, were part of the inner defense line round Japan itself and represented an ideal base for American strategic bombers. By May 1944 Toyoda had dispatched the carriers to join Ozawa, despite their lack of trained air groups, and had concentrated a total of 1700

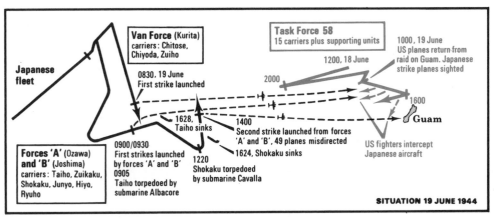

Van Force (Kurita)
carriers: Chitose, Chiyoda, Zuiho

Task Force 58
15 carriers plus supporting units

1000, 19 June
US planes return from raid on Guam. Japanese strike planes sighted

1200, 18 June

2000

Japanese fleet

0830, 19 June
First strike launched

1628, Taiho sinks

1400
Second strike launched from forces 'A' and 'B', 49 planes misdirected

1600

Guam

Forces 'A' (Ozawa) **and 'B'** (Joshima)
carriers: Taiho, Zuikaku, Shokaku, Junyo, Hiyo, Ryuho

0900/0930
First strikes launched by forces 'A' and 'B'
0905
Taiho torpedoed by submarine Albacore

1220
Shokaku torpedoed by submarine Cavalla

1624, Shokaku sinks

US fighters intercept Japanese aircraft

SITUATION 19 JUNE 1944

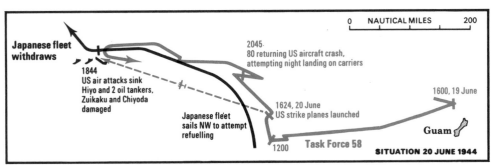

Japanese fleet withdraws

1844
US air attacks sink Hiyo and 2 oil tankers, Zuikaku and Chiyoda damaged

2045.
80 returning US aircraft crash, attempting night landing on carriers

0   NAUTICAL MILES   200

Japanese fleet sails NW to attempt refuelling

1624, 20 June
US strike planes launched

1600, 19 June

1200   **Task Force 58**   **Guam**

SITUATION 20 JUNE 1944

16 June
TG 58.1 and 58.4 make air strikes

IWO JIMA

Formosa

PHILIPPINE ISLANDS

Luzon

Japanese 1st Mobile Fleet (Ozawa)

NEGROS

PANAY

Mindanao

TAWITAWI

PALAU

Japanese Southern Force (Ugaki)

HALMAHERA

BATJAN

Celebes

NEW GUINEA

1030, 18 June
All task groups rendezvous

Marianas Islands

SAIPAN
TINIAN

13/15 June
TG 58.2, 3 and 7 ('Battle Line') attack Jap positions and airfields prior to landings

GUAM

12 June

Task Force 58 (Mitscher)

1700, 16 June
Japanese fleets rendezvous for refuelling

YAP

WOLEAI

TRUK

0   NAUTICAL MILES   600

aircraft at shore bases in the Dutch East Indies, the Philippines, New Guinea and the Bismarks. As American intentions became clear, more than 500 of these machines were moved forward into the Marianas.

This was the first Japanese mistake, for while Vice-Admiral Richmond Turner's Amphibious Force prepared for the assault on Saipan, set for 15 June, the carriers of Task Force 58 roamed far and wide, hitting Japanese bases. After neutralizing strikes against Palau, Yap and Woleai in late March, they moved southward to support MacArthur in Hollandia and, on their return to the Central Pacific in May, pounded Truk, Marcus and Wake Islands. At

the same time, shore-based bombers hit the by-passed Marshall Islands of Jaluit and Wotje. Japanese aircraft and installations were destroyed in each attack, gradually undermining Toyoda's plan. The process reached a climax on 11, 12 and 13 June as Mitscher's force moved in to soften up the Marianas and interdict Japanese supply routes through the islands of Chichi Jima and Iwo Jima, 650 miles to the north. By the time the Marines invaded Saipan, the 500 aircraft in the Marianas had been largely eliminated, complete American air superiority achieved and one of the main elements of Operation A-Go had effectively been destroyed.

Top left: The positions of the US and Japanese Fleet on 19 June 1944.

Above left: The position on 20 June as the Japanese withdrew.

Above: The journey of both fleets to the Philippine Sea.

Left: Vice-Admiral Marc Mitscher commander of Task Force 58, off Saipan.

Right: Admiral Richmond
'Kelly' Turner off Kwajalein
during an earlier operation
to take the Marshall Islands.

Neither Toyoda nor Ozawa was aware of the true state of air losses (the local commander neglected to tell them for fear of repercussions), and when the decision to seek battle was taken on 13 June, both retained a degree of optimism about its outcome. Practical problems continued to emerge, forcing changes to the original plan. In late May the defenders of the island of Biak, an important air base in the efforts to halt MacArthur's advance, had called urgently for aid, and a special naval force under Vice-Admiral Matome Ugaki, composed of the battleships *Yamato* and *Musashi* with cruisers and destroyers, had been detached from Ozawa's command. This had now to be recalled and directed to rendezvous with the rest of the fleet in the Philippine Sea, a maneuver which was to take time and preclude the original scheme whereby it was 'to lure the enemy fleet.' The two forces met on 16 June, but surprise was quickly lost. American submarines saw and reported both portions, allowing Vice-Admiral Raymond Spruance time to assess the danger and make the necessary dispositions. The last great carrier battle was about to begin.

On the American side, Spruance realized that the Japanese could not approach to within range until 19 June, and was not prepared to

Right: Admiral Richmond 'Kelly' Turner off Kwajalein during an earlier operation to take the Marshall Islands.

Right: The team which was in charge of operations in the Central Pacific. Left to right: Rear Admiral Kelly Turner, Vice-Admiral Raymond Spruance, Admiral Nimitz, Lieutenant General Richardson, Major General Ralph Smith, Major General 'Howling Mad' Smith, Rear Admiral McMorris.

advance far into the Philippine Sea to meet them. His first duty was the protection of Turner's Amphibious Force, so he ordered his carriers to complete their neutralization of Japanese bases on Guam, Tinian, Chichi Jima and Iwo Jima before rendezvousing 180 miles west of the Marianas on the evening of 18 June. Once assembled, Task Force 58 was formidable. Its 15 carriers were divided into four self-contained task groups (TG 58-1 comprising *Hornet*, *Yorktown*, *Belleau Wood* and *Bataan*; TG 58-2 *Bunker Hill*, *Wasp*, *Monterey* and *Cabot*; TG 58-3 *Enterprise*, *Lexington*, *Princeton* and *San Jacinto*; TG 58-4 *Essex*, *Langley* and *Cowpens*), each with its complement of battleships, cruisers and destroyers, and the total air strength exceeded 900, the majority of which were fighters and dive or torpedo bombers. In normal circumstances the task groups would have fought as separate entities, but with the prospect of a major fleet action, Spruance altered their organization. The battleships of the carrier group escorts were formed into a 'Battle Line' (known as TG 58-7) under Vice-Admiral Willis Lee with four heavy cruisers and 13 destroyers transferred from Turner's Amphibious Force as an escort. This was pushed forward 15 miles ahead of the carriers to act as a shield, with TG 58-4 in attendance

to give air cover, while the other three carrier groups were stationed in a north-south line some 15 miles apart. It was basically a defensive formation, designed to trap and destroy incoming Japanese air or surface assaults.

Meanwhile Ozawa's force continued to approach the Marianas from the west. It was organized into three parts. A Force, under Ozawa himself, was centered upon the three big fleet carriers *Taiho*, *Zuikaku* and *Shokaku*, with a screen of cruisers and destroyers and provided the main air strength with 207 aircraft. B Force, commanded by Rear Admiral Joshima, contained the slower fleet carriers *Junyo* and *Hiyo* as well as the light carrier *Ryuho*, which between them mustered 135 aircraft. It was protected by one battleship, one cruiser and nine destroyers. These two groups operated independently about 12 miles apart, while C or Van Force under Vice-Admiral Kurita, comprising the four battleships *Yamato*, *Musashi*, *Haruna* and *Kongo*, four heavy cruisers, a light cruiser and nine destroyers, screening three light carriers *Chitose*, *Chiyoda* and *Zuiho* with a combined complement of 90 aircraft, sailed about a 100 miles in advance to draw the fire of enemy air strikes and extend the range of reconnaissance seaplanes.

In fact it was in the area of reconnaissance

Left: Spruance and Holland Smith during the invasion of Saipan.

that the Japanese enjoyed about their only advantage, for their float-planes, catapulted from battleships and cruisers, had a greater endurance than their American counterparts. Because of this Ozawa was aware of Spruance's dispositions on 18 June and in a position to plan a strike, at a range of approximately 350 miles, for dawn the next day. Spruance, on the other hand, with reconnaissance aircraft that reached the limit of their fuel about 60 miles short of the Japanese fleet, spent 18 June in

Left: On a mission to bomb Saipan, a Republic P-47 of the 7th Air Force warms up on a catapult prior to launching on the USS *Manila Bay*.

ignorance of enemy movements, his latest reports having come in 24 hours earlier from the submarine *Cavalla*, shadowing A Force. It was not until 1000 hours on 19 June, when the radar of Lee's Battle Line detected a swarm of incoming aircraft, that the Americans were able to react. Even so, they managed to inflict the first casualties, for as Ozawa's A Force launched its strike aircraft, the submarine *Albacore* mounted a surprise assault, damaging the carrier *Taiho*. It was but a foretaste of things to come.

As soon as the Japanese air armada, divided into three waves and comprising nearly 250 assorted dive bombers, torpedo bombers and fighters, was detected, the American carriers turned together into the wind, launched any bombers or torpedo aircraft on deck, sending them out of the way to the eastward, and concentrated solely upon fighters. Nearly 300 Hellcats took to the air, some of them flying over Guam to attack the few shore-based air-

Left: Gunners of the 805th Engineer Aviation Battalion firing .5 caliber from the deck of a Landing Ship Tank during the journey to Saipan.

89

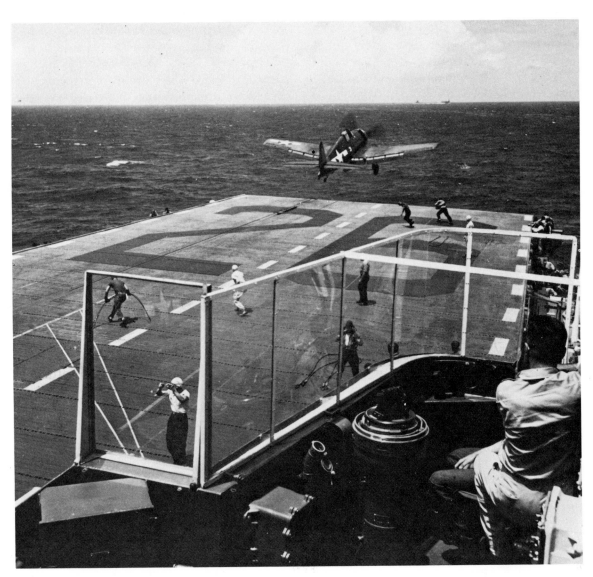

Left: A Grumman F6F Hellcat is catapulted off the USS *Monterey* during the Battle of the Philippine Sea. The *Monterey* was an *Independence* Class carrier, which was never intended as more than a stopgap but saw valiant service as a night carrier during the final stages of the Pacific War.

craft which the Japanese brought into the battle, but the vast majority advancing to intercept Ozawa's carrier strikes. These interceptions, which continued throughout the morning, usually took place some 45 to 60 miles in front of the American fleet and were so successful that they soon became known as 'The Great Marianas Turkey Shoot.' In the first Japanese wave, from C Force, out of 69 aircraft 42 were destroyed and none penetrated to the American ships. Of the second wave, comprising 128 planes from A Force, more than 100 were intercepted and shot down. The remainder broke through to face the massed gunfire of the Battle Line, and an even smaller remnant managed to reach the aircraft carriers beyond. Minor damage was inflicted upon the *Wasp* and *Bunker Hill* of TG 58-2, but by 1200 hours it was all over. Less than 30 survivors limped back to the Japanese fleet with dangerously exaggerated tales of American carriers on fire and sinking. Meanwhile, the third wave, comprising 47 aircraft from B Force, had flown too far to the north. Just over half of them failed to make any contact with the Americans, returning to their carriers unmolested, but the others succeeded in locating the most northerly task group, where they were pounced on by patrolling Hellcats. Seven of the Japanese aircraft were destroyed: the rest dumped their bombs ineffectively and fled. The Americans let them go.

But if Spruance was unable to hit the source of the Japanese air strikes, the same was not the case with his submarines, and as the morning came to an end a double disaster was inflicted by them upon Ozawa. At 1220 hours the *Cavalla*, after having lost contact with A Force during 18 June, suddenly found herself in an ideal position to attack the *Shokaku*.

Left: Grumman TBF Avengers and Curtiss SB2C Helldivers en route to attack Japanese carriers in the Philippine Sea.

Three torpedoes tore into her side, starting fires which the crew tried desperately to fight for nearly three hours. But their efforts were in vain: at the end of that time gasoline vapor exploded and the *Shokaku*, one of the last remaining elements of Nagumo's Pearl Harbor force, went to the bottom. At almost the same time the *Taiho*, apparently undamaged by *Albacore*'s earlier attack, also exploded when fumes from a ruptured fuel system ignited. Ozawa's best ships had gone down.

In the meantime, further Japanese air strikes, launched from the *Zuikaku* of A Force and the three light carriers of B Force, tried to break through to the American ships. Of the planes involved, only about half located the southern carrier task group and were promptly hit by waiting Hellcats. Few of the Japanese machines survived. The remainder, 49 strong, headed for Guam to refuel before restarting their search. But they were unaware of the true state of affairs on the island, dominated by the Americans since dawn. Set upon by 27 Hellcats, 30 Japanese planes were shot down over the sea or as they tried to land on the battered airstrip. By 1600 hours the Americans had cleared the air entirely of enemy machines and, except for action against the occasional shore-based raider, no more air fighting took

A Grumman F6F Hellcat about to take off from the flight deck of the new carrier *Yorktown* (CV-10). It was named after the carrier sunk at Midway.

place on 19 June. The Japanese air arm had been all but destroyed. Of the 373 aircraft sent out from Ozawa's carriers, only 130 had returned; a figure which dropped to 102 as pilot inexperience showed itself in a series of crashes as the survivors relanded. In addition, about 50 land-based aircraft had been destroyed. Such losses were irreplaceable: Japan would be unable to man or equip an effective carrier force again. American losses, by way of comparison, had been only 29 aircraft. Spruance's defensive stance had been more than justified.

But the Battle of the Philippine Sea was not over, for the Americans, brought up to believe that no naval action could be termed a success without the destruction of the enemy fleet, were determined to go over to the offensive. This was not possible immediately, however, as Spruance was still not aware of Ozawa's position. In fact the American Task Force had drifted eastward during the air battle, increasing the distance between the two fleets to something like 400 miles, outside the range of Mitscher's strike aircraft. Therefore, as a first move, Task Force 58 had to turn westward to try and close the gap while sending out reconnaissance missions in all directions. No sign of the Japanese was reported during the remainder of 19 June, and it began to look as if Ozawa had escaped.

If the Japanese commander had realized the full state of his losses there is little doubt that he would have withdrawn swiftly to Japan, but

Ozawa was unaware of the extent of his defeat. Not only did he believe the stories brought back to him about American aircraft and carriers destroyed, but he was also convinced that many of his missing strike planes had landed on Guam or neighboring islands and were ready to take to the air again. As a result, on 20 June, having withdrawn northwestward to rendezvous with replenishment tankers he was prepared to renew the battle at the earliest opportunity. It was only when his communications staff intercepted a signal from an American aircraft at 1615 hours on 20 June, reporting contact with the Japanese fleet, that worries began to arise. Refueling was postponed and Ozawa retired still further northwestward, hoping to outpace the Americans before nightfall and so avoid an air strike which, with only 100 operational aircraft left, he would be unable to counter.

The carrier USS *Manila Bay* under attack by four Japanese aircraft.

He very nearly succeeded. When the
Americans received the long-awaited signal of
contact at about 1600 hours, the chances of
putting in a successful strike were slim. The
enemy fleet was only just within range and,
even if aircraft were launched immediately
they would have to be relanded after dark, a
procedure for which the American pilots were
not trained. But Spruance and Mitscher were
not going to let the opportunity slip by, and
within half an hour of the reported sighting 77
Dauntless dive bombers, 54 Avenger torpedo
bombers and 85 Hellcat fighters had taken to
the air, heading west into the setting sun. Their
mission was a resounding success. After a section broke away to deal with Ozawa's refueling
force of six tankers, the remainder swept aside
the thin screen of Zero fighter protection and
pounded the Japanese fleet, concentrating
upon the carriers. After 20 minutes of frenetic
action the *Hiyo* had been torpedoed and sunk,
the *Zuikaku* crippled, the *Chiyoda* set on fire,
the battleship *Haruna* and cruiser *Maya*
damaged. In addition, a further 65 planes of
the Japanese naval air arm had been destroyed, leaving Ozawa with less than 40 operational machines. Admitting defeat at last, he
fled to Okinawa. American losses were slight,

for although nearly 80 of the returning aircraft crashed as they tried to reland after nightfall, few crew members were killed. Indeed, after widespread rescue operations only 16 pilots and 33 aircrew were reported missing. The Battle of the Philippine Sea – an American victory of epic proportions – was over. The Japanese naval air arm had been destroyed and her carriers were reduced to impotence denied the ability either to strike or to defend

Below: During the Battle of the Philippine Sea the invasion of Saipan proceeded. The 5th Marines landed south of Garapan on 15 June 1944 and set about clearing the northern half of the island. In this picture the Marines are crawling their way to their assigned positions under heavy enemy fire.

themselves in future battles. American naval and air superiority was virtually complete – the final naval battle of the Pacific War, at Leyte Gulf in October 1944, was needed to eliminate the Japanese fleet entirely – and the inexorable advances upon the Japanese homeland could continue virtually unopposed. The lesson was clear: in naval as in land warfare in the twentieth century, air power was the essential key to victory.

Right: Marines use a tank as a shield as they come ashore.

General MacArthur leads his entourage back to the Philippines, fulfilling the promise 'I shall return' made almost three years earlier. On the extreme left of the picture is Sergio Osmena who was to be the first President of an independent Philippines.

6 LEYTE GULF
The Greatest Naval Battle Ever

The Battle of Leyte Gulf marks the end of an era in several respects. Not only was it the Japanese Navy's last engagement as an independent fighting force, and the last major naval encounter of World War II, but it was also the last great sea battle fought to date. Appropriately enough, it has the additional distinction of being the largest naval battle in history, one in which every weapon except the mine was employed on both sides. Leyte Gulf saw too the introduction of Japan's new desperate, and deadly, air tactic – the famous kamikaze suicide plane.

As agreed by Churchill and Roosevelt in the early stages of the war, the American Joint Chiefs of Staff directed the war effort in the Pacific theater, the British controlled the Middle East and India, while Europe and the Atlantic were under joint Anglo-American command. After the Battle of Midway, two commanders came to dominate the American war in the Pacific: General Douglas MacArthur and Admiral Chester Nimitz.

Nimitz held the Central Pacific Command. The Navy saw the action in the Pacific as es-

Above right: Admiral Soemu Toyoda, Commander in Chief of the Combined Fleet, in September 1944. Toyoda believed the Battle of Leyte Gulf would be a 'Decisive Battle' but what he did not realize was that it would signify the decisive end of the Japanese Imperial Fleet.

Right: Rear Admirals Jesse Oldendorf (left) and Thomas Kinkaid (center) played crucial roles at Leyte Gulf.

sentially its bailiwick – Europe was the Army's war – and was determined to have the deciding voice in setting policy. Nimitz and the Naval Chief of Staff, Admiral Ernest King, wanted to launch an amphibious campaign west from Hawaii across the central Pacific to Japan, via the Gilbert, Marshall, Caroline, and Mariana Islands, arguing that no one would be safe until the 'spider web' Japan had established throughout Micronesia had been swept up. Their particular concern was to avoid putting Navy forces under the Army's command.

That, of course, was just what MacArthur was asking for. As Commander in the Southwest Pacific area – Australia, New Guinea, the Philippines, and most of the Netherlands East Indies – he planned to launch his own drive to Japan via New Guinea and the Philippines. Further, he proposed that the entire Pacific fleet be placed under his command to cover his advance along the 'New Guinea-Mindanao Axis.' There was no way he would accept the purely defensive role laid out for him by Nimitz and King.

In effect, MacArthur and Nimitz were com-

Above left: An early picture Thomas Kinkaid. He was Commander of the 7th Fleet at Leyte Gulf.

Left: Kinkaid with Lieutenant General Walter Krueger, Commander of the 6th Army, as they head for the Philippines.

Left: The heavy cruiser
Portland fires her forward
8-inch guns during the Leyte
landings in October 1944.

peting to see who could defeat Japan first. Far from disapproving of this interservice rivalry, President Franklin Roosevelt actually encouraged it. The Commander in Chief believed that the competition would spur each side on to greater efforts and produce faster results. Unfortunately the situation got out of hand, and was to have an important effect on the Battle of Leyte Gulf. The Navy's hatred of MacArthur was so open and virulent that it 'seemed childish,' according to Secretary of War, Henry Stimson. MacArthur later wrote that 'of all the faulty decisions of the war, perhaps the most inexpressible one was the failure to unify the command in the Pacific . . .' – though what he meant, of course, was the failure to unify command under *his* direction.

It must be noted, however, that if the rift between MacArthur and Nimitz was as wide as some analysts have described, American efforts in the Pacific would have been paralyzed and the war there would never have been won. In fact, the two had much in common: highly-trained minds that could cut through non-essentials to reach the heart of a problem; the ability to instill tremendous loyalty in their men; and above all, the will to win. Although they honestly differed in their views on the best way to win the Pacific war, a great deal of mutual respect and a high degree of co-operation kept the operation running fairly smoothly. When Nimitz needed air support from long-range, land-based bombers, Mac-Arthur provided it, and when the general needed carriers or other naval vessels, he borrowed them from the admiral. In other words, neither ever allowed differences of opinion over strategy to deflect him from his primary objective – to defeat the Japanese.

By the beginning of 1943 the Americans had gained control of southeastern New Guinea, Guadalcanal, and Tulagi, and had definitely gained the initiative in the Southwest Pacific.

MacArthur was leading one wing of a two-pronged attack, moving along the north coast of New Guinea toward the Philippines. His strategy was based on achieving local air superiority with land-based planes to cover his advancing troops, and on isolating each successive Japanese base before subjecting it to the final air, ground, and naval assault. His 'island-hopping' program had been successful, but had also proved too slow, so he devised 'leap-frogging' tactics. This involved striking where the Japanese were weakest ('hitting them where they ain't') and bypassing the stronger garrisons, leaving them to wither away, isolated from supplies and reinforcements.

Nimitz, meanwhile, was striking across the Pacific, through the Marshalls, Marianas, and Palaus, toward Iwo Jima and Okinawa. His offensive was based on a combination of fast carrier task forces and hard-hitting amphibious groups. Carrier-based planes would knock out Japanese air defenses over the island target; fleets would move in to blast the shore defenses; and finally Marines and soldiers would land to overcome the last resistance. Once an island was secured, airfields would be established, the Navy would build up harbor and supply facilities, and the whole island would be turned into a forward supply base for the capture of the next objective.

The methods used in both areas involved months of hard, bloody, dangerous fighting – but they worked. By June 1944 Nimitz had worked his way through the Marshalls and Gilberts and was ready to attack Saipan, the key Japanese fortress in the Marianas. Imperial General Headquarters quite rightly decided to meet the attack with the full force of the Japanese fleet. Not only would the loss of

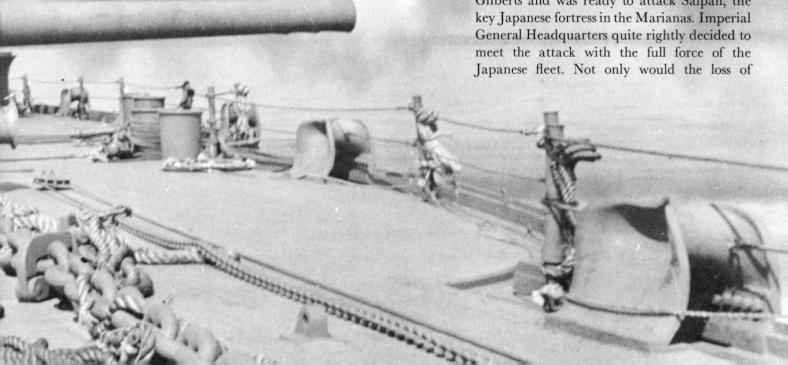

Right: The monster battleship *Yamato* is hit by a bomb on its forecastle as it crosses the Sibuyan Sea on its way to the San Bernardino Strait.

Below right: A Japanese warship is attacked by American bombers off the Philippines.

Below far right: A cruiser comes alongside the badly damaged carrier *Princeton*, part of Task Force 38. The Princeton's avgas supply was hit and the fires were uncontrollable so the ship was sunk on 25 October.

Saipan sever their communications with Japanese forces in the south, but the island's position only 1350 miles from Tokyo would make it an ideal base for long-range bomber strikes against the Home Islands. In the greatest air battle of the war, 15 American carriers with 900 planes met nine Japanese carriers with 370 planes. During 'The Great Marianas Turkey Shoot' the Japanese lost 315 of those planes, a carrier, and several battleships and cruisers. The losses in planes, and especially in pilots, were irreplaceable at that stage in the war; the fall of Saipan showed the prospect of defeat so clearly that it led to the fall of General Hideki Tojo's war government.

At the end of July, MacArthur had gained control of New Guinea and was poised to cross the Celebes Sea to Mindanao, but the argument on future strategy was still fiercely contested. King and most other Navy planners in Washington wanted to bypass the Philippines in favor of an attack on Formosa or even the Home Islands themselves. MacArthur waxed eloquent on the need to recapture the major part of the Philippines – partly for strategic reasons, but primarily because he had given his word to return. Failure to do so, he maintained, would compromise American honor and prestige in the Far East for many years to come. Nimitz was in the middle. He took a dim view of skipping over the Philippines altogether, but was willing to consider bypassing Luzon if major air and naval bases could be established in the central and southern Philippines.

The stalemate seemed unresolvable when President Roosevelt intervened and decided to have a meeting with Nimitz and MacArthur at Pearl Harbor to discuss the next moves. During the meeting on 26 and 27 July, MacArthur and Nimitz talked while the President and the others listened. In the end, all were convinced of the merits of MacArthur's 'Leyte then Luzon' concept. In September the Allied Combined Chiefs of Staff, meeting at the Octagon Conference in Quebec, agreed that MacArthur and Nimitz should converge on Leyte in December, but within a week Admiral William Halsey, who had sent out task forces of his Third Fleet headed by the new Essex class fast carriers to soften up Morotai, Yap, and the Palau Islands, reported meeting few Japanese planes and no warships. His story of the 'amazing and fantastic' lack of Japanese resistance put a different light on the matter. Without opposition, MacArthur's forces could make one long hop from New Guinea to Leyte, by-passing Mindanao completely. In an unusual example of strategic flexibility the Octagon Conference moved the date of the Leyte Mission up to 20 October.

By this time the Japanese were in grave difficulty, despite their many advantages, largely because Imperial General Headquarters had been operating with an outdated concept of war. For example, although the Japanese could and did design better warships and airplanes than the Americans, they did not give naval airpower – the weapon upon which their defense should have relied – top priority. During 1943 America built 22 aircraft carriers; Japan produced only three and never managed to recruit enough pilots to man even a restricted air arm. Japan controlled 80 percent of the world's rubber along with vast quantities of oil, tin, tungsten, manganese, and

iron ore – but had no way to exploit those resources. A large merchant fleet was needed, but battleships had been given priority over an expanded merchant navy. By 1943 Japan was already facing a severe oil shortage and curtailed naval operations because it no longer had the tanker capacity to transport the oil from the Netherlands East Indies. As a result of this basic economic weakness in their defense structure, the Japanese had been grimly hanging on since their defeat in Guadalcanal and Papua. Instead of fighting to win, they were now simply trying to hold on as long as possible.

Of all the services the newest, the naval air arm, suffered most. Between 1942 and 1944 Japan lost 8000 navy planes and enormous numbers of pilots. The planes could be replaced, albeit with difficulty, but the men could not. Casualties increased as the quality of new recruits and training procedures fell. With the death of Admiral Isoroku Yamamoto, the major supporter of naval air power was

gone and the navy soon returned to its first love, the battleship.

By March 1944 Japanese strategists could foresee the American invasion of the Philippines, long before Allied planners had managed to agree on it themselves. Japan was most concerned with holding Luzon, thus maintaining communication with Malaya and Indonesia. But she had to be prepared to defend not only all the Philippine Islands, but Formosa and the Ryukyus as well; if the inner defense line that extended from the Kuriles through the Home Islands to the Philippines was breached, Japan would lose her lines of communication through the Formosa Straits and the South China Sea and all the resources of the southern colonies, and would be forced to fall back on the resources of China alone.

In July/August 1944, then, Japanese planners drew up four separate *Sho* (or victory) plans. *Sho-1* covered the Philippines while the others concerned Formosa-Ryukyas, Honshu-Kyushu, and Hokkaido-Kuriles. *Sho-1* was a typically Japanese plan that employed divided forces, diversions, unexpected attacks, and an elaborate time schedule. First the Northern Force under Admiral Ozawa, built around the four carriers *Zuikaku*, *Zuiho*, *Chitose*, and *Chiyoda*, would lure the main American force – Halsey's Third Fleet – to the north, away from the real objective. Then the Center Force commanded by Admiral Kurita, consisting of the giant battleships *Yamato* and *Musashi*, nine cruisers, and a destroyer screen, would come south of Luzon through the San Bernardino Strait into Leyte Gulf. At the same time Admiral Nishimura's Southern Force would move up on the gulf through the Surigao Strait between Leyte and Mindanao. The two forces would converge, destroy shipping in the gulf, smash the Allied bridgehead, and presumably depart before the Third Fleet could return. The carriers were being used as decoys because the naval air force had already been virtually eliminated – there were only 116 planes on Ozawa's four carriers, and less than 200 in

land-based air groups in the Ryukyus, Formosa, and Manila. If the plan succeeded the American army at Leyte would be destroyed as completely as the navy had been three years earlier at Pearl Harbor, and Japan would have gained at least a year's breathing space.

Ideally, *Sho-1* would be timed to catch the Leyte landings in their 'naked' stage, as troops and equipment were being launched. But Japan's oil shortage was so great that if *Sho-1* was activated too soon, the ships would be short of fuel for the real engagement. Japanese intelligence had predicted a landing at Leyte during the last ten days of October, but could be certain of neither the time nor the place. Thus the Commander in Chief of the Combined Fleet, Admiral Soemu Toyoda, had to wait until American ships were actually seen entering Leyte Gulf before activating the plan. He was taking a last desperate gamble – that his forces, free from air attack, could make contact with the enemy and destroy them with overwhelming gun power. The Combined Fleet would probably be destroyed. But if the Philippines were lost, and Japan cut off from her only supply of oil, the fleet would be immobilized anyway. In other words, *Sho-1* was a huge kamikaze operation.

Allied preparations for the Leyte landing began in September, immediately after the schedule was advanced by the Octagon Conference. Morotai was taken, to become a staging base for short-range fighters and light and medium bombers. Early in October, Mac-Arthur's forces and those of the US Seventh Fleet under Admiral Thomas Kinkaid began to gather along the shores of New Guinea. The invasion group, when finally assembled, would contain 738 ships including 157 combat vessels, 420 amphibians, 73 service ships, and 84 patrol boats, as well as mine sweeping and hydrographic specialist craft. Supporting the convoy was Halsey's Third Fleet – 17 carriers, six battleships, 17 cruisers, and 64 destroyers. Altogether it was the most powerful naval force ever assembled (though not as large as the force that would attack Okinawa the following April). On 10 October the mine sweepers began to lead the enormous convoy away from the New Guinea coast, toward the island of Leyte.

Between 12-14 October a major air attack was launched against Formosa; although Japan's weakness in the air had made the giant hop from New Guinea to Leyte possible, it was still necessary to destroy what remained of her land-based air power. Vice-Admiral Marc Mitscher, Commander of Task Force 38 which was part of the Third Fleet, sent a host of planes from his nine carriers against the island. More than 200 Japanese fighters rose to meet them but, as their commander Admiral Fukudome later lamented, they were 'nothing but so many eggs thrown against the wall . . . .' More than a third were lost on 12 October alone. Overall, Task Force 38 destroyed more than 500 Japanese planes and 40 transports and other vessels. A series of raids by China-based B-29s wreaked even more havoc on the island.

During the next week Japanese air bases in Luzon, Mindanao, and the Netherlands East Indies were attacked from the air, and a naval force was sent against the Kurile Islands. There was little resistance from the Japanese,

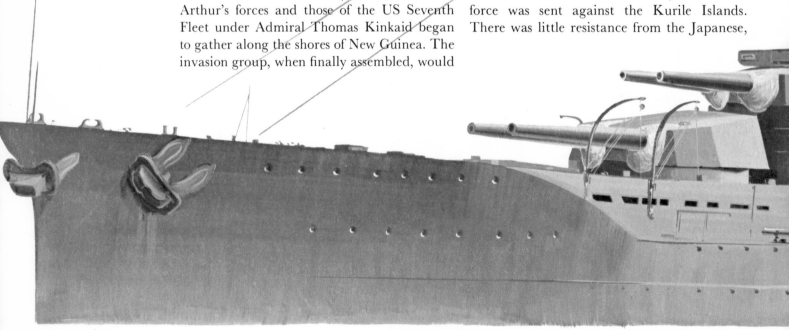

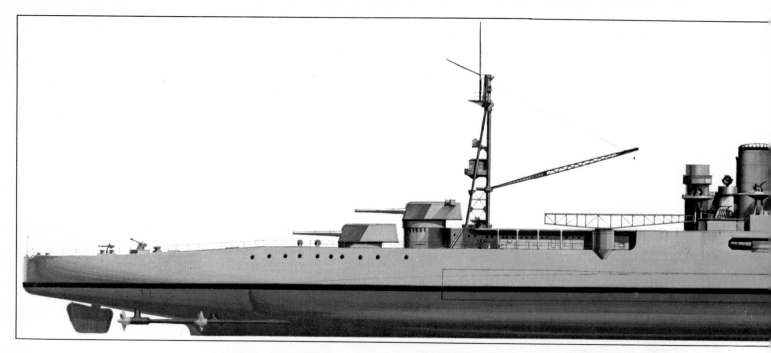

Right: A crew member on an
escort carrier stands by as a
Japanese bomb explodes
nearby.

who were hoarding their planes for the 'general decisive battle' ahead.

For once the Allies had no advance knowledge of Japanese plans. MacArthur's staff discounted the idea that Japan might oppose the landings. General George Kenney, Commander of the Far East Army Air Forces considered that Leyte would be 'relatively undefended,' and on 20 October MacArthur's headquarters announced that the Japanese Navy would not use the San Bernardino or Surigao Straits because of navigational hazards and lack of space to maneuver. Admiral Halsey hoped very much that the Japanese

fleet would come out and fight, but was not at all certain it would.

Events during the main landings did not dispel this view. The mine sweepers had reached the entrances of Leyte Gulf on 17 October. By midday on 18 October the four islands (Dinagat, Calicoan, Suluan, and Homonhon) that mark the entrance to Leyte Gulf from the Philippine Sea had been taken by the 6th Ranger Infantry Battalion under Lieutenant Colonel H A Mucci. Rear Admiral Jesse Oldendorf had moved his fire support ships into the gulf and was bombarding the southern landing beaches to cover the under-

Above: The heavy cruiser *Takao* displaced 13,160 tons and carried ten 8-inch guns. She was part of Kurita's Force A but had to retire to Singapore after suffering damage off Palawan.

Left: The USS *Heermann* lays a smoke screen off Samar on 25 October 1944.

water demolition teams. Bombardments continued through the next day, while planes from three groups of escort carriers (usually known as Taffy 1, Taffy 2, and Taffy 3) commanded by Rear Admiral Thomas Sprague attacked Japanese airfields and defenses on Leyte, Mindanao, and in the Visayans.

A-Day, 20 October, dawned with perfect weather and light surf. The fire support ships began their preliminary bombardment at 0700 hours and the troops began landing on schedule at 1000 hours, meeting only light mortar fire. After the first wave had landed, the moment for which MacArthur had been waiting for two and a half years arrived. Accompanied by Sergio Osmena, who had become President of the Philippines following the death of Manuel Quezon, the general embarked in a landing craft, got out into the water, and strode ashore. Standing on the beach, in a downpour of rain, he broadcast a message to the Philippine people: 'People of the Philippines, I have returned. By the grace of Almighty God, our forces stand again on Philippine soil – soil consecrated by the blood of our two peoples.' He urged the Filipinos to 'rally to me ... In the name of your sacred dead, strike! Let no heart be faint. Let every arm be

Left: The USS *St Lo*, an
escort carrier, is hit by a
kamikaze aircraft.

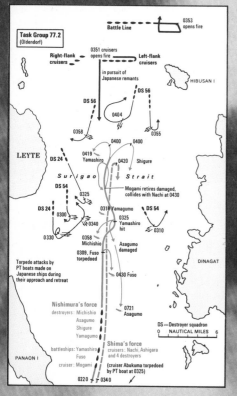

Left: The Battle of Surigao
Strait.

steeled.' His words had an overwhelming impact in the Philippines and he urged Roosevelt, in a note dramatically scribbled out on the beach, to grant the Philippines independence immediately after the successful liberation campaign.

By midnight on 21 October, 132,000 men and 200,000 tons of equipment had been landed on Leyte; the airfields at Dulag and Tacloban, as well as the docking facilities in Tacloban town, were in American hands. By 22 October the amphibious portion of the operation was over. Of the hundreds of ships that had jammed the Leyte Gulf, only 28 Liberty Ships and 25 Landing Ships Medium (LSMs) and Landing Ship Tanks (LSTs) remained. On land, General Walter Krueger and the Sixth Army remained to root out the 60,000 Japanese who were still fiercely defending the island.

All this time there had been no sign of the Japanese fleet, and it looked as if the predictions of a virtually uncontested operation had come true. But in fact, Toyoda had only been informed on 17 October that the Allies were approaching Leyte Gulf, and had activated *Sho-1*. The next day Kurita's main battle force left Lingga Roads. On 20 October, after stopping for fuel at Brunei Bay in North Borneo, the force split. Kurita, with five battleships and most of the heavy cruisers, headed for the Sibuyan Sea and the San Bernardino Strait. Nishimura's Southern Force crossed the Sulu Sea heading toward the Surigao Strait, supported by two heavy cruisers, a light cruiser, and seven destroyers – all under the command of Admiral Shima. Meanwhile, Ozawa and the Northern Carrier Force had slipped out of the Inland Sea on their decoy mission.

At 0116 hours on 23 October two American submarines, *Darter* and *Dace*, who were patrolling the Palawan Passage between Palawan Island and the South China Sea, made radar contact with Kurita's Center Force. They sent off a report to Halsey, who received it gladly at 0620 hours; it was the first news he had of Center Force since it left Lingga. Twelve minutes later, *Darter* emptied her bow torpedo tubes at the heavy cruiser *Atago*, Kurita's flagship, which sank almost immediately. The two submarines managed to sink another heavy cruiser and put a third out of commission before the day had ended. Early the next

morning, however, *Darter* ran hard aground in the difficult channel and had to be abandoned. Kurita, who had swum over and raised his flag in the giant battleship *Yamato*, took Center Force on into the Sibuyan Sea.

The submarine's timely warning had enabled Halsey to prepare a warm reception for Kurita, and by noon on 24 October he had deployed three of Task Force 38's fast carrier groups on a broad front: Rear Admiral Fred Sherman's group in the north, Rear Admiral Bogan's off the San Bernardino Strait, and Rear Admiral Davison's off Samar. Sherman was in the best position to damage Kurita, but before any of the groups could launch a strike, three waves of 50 to 60 Japanese planes each flew in from Luzon armed with bombs and torpedoes. Although many were shot down, one dive bomber broke through the anti-aircraft fire, escaped the Combat Air Patrol, and hit the light carrier *Princeton* which sank later that day.

Bogan and Davison were able to launch attacks, and since most of the Japanese planes were busy attacking Sherman, the Americans were able to hit Center Force hard. The great battleship *Musashi* sustained hits from 19 torpedoes and 17 bombs, and sank with most of her crew.

At 1400 hours, Kurita, his repeated requests for air cover denied, pulled the Japanese ships west to regroup and assess damages; with four battleships, six heavy cruisers, two light cruisers, and ten destroyers left, Center Force was still a formidable force. Kurita asked permission to wait until nightfall before running the San Bernardino Strait, but Toyoda ordered him straight ahead. The Battle of the Sibuyan Sea had put him seven hours behind schedule and there was already no way he could keep his dawn rendezvous in Leyte Gulf with Nishimura and the Southern Force.

Meanwhile, while Kurita was fighting in the Sibuyan Sea, Southern Force was making its own way toward Leyte Gulf. Nishimura's squadron – the battleships *Fuso* and *Yamashiro*, the heavy cruiser *Mogami*, and four destroyers – was in the lead, with Shima's supporting force several hours behind. They were first sighted by planes from the carriers *Enterprise* and *Franklin* at 0905 hours on 24 October. Admiral Kinkaid of the Seventh Fleet correctly estimated that the Japanese force inten-

Right: Admiral William Halsey, whose mad dash to deal with Ozawa's decoy fleet nearly ended in disaster at Leyte Gulf.

Below: The Japanese battleship *Kongo* was rebuilt between 1933 and 1940 to act as a carrier escort. She was part of Kurita's Force A and survived the Battle of Leyte Gulf only to be torpedoed and sunk off Formosa in November 1944.

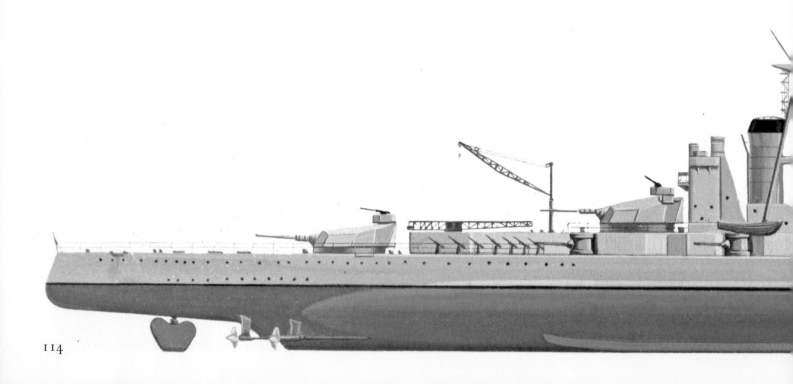

ded to break into the Gulf via the Surigao Strait that night, and shortly after noon had alerted every ship under his command to prepare for the attack. At 1830 hours Nishimura knew that Kurita would not be able to rendezvous as scheduled; nevertheless, when he received a message from Toyoda about an hour later directing that 'all forces will dash to the attack, trusting in divine guidance,' he pushed on toward the strait without even waiting for Shima to catch up. Without air cover, the only chance he believed he had lay in getting into the Gulf under cover of darkness.

But Kinkaid and Rear Admiral Oldendorf, who commanded the Bombardment and Fire Support Group from the heavy cruiser *Louisville*, had laid a neat trap for anyone who tried to enter the gulf that night. Six battleships, four heavy cruisers, and four light cruisers were deployed along a 15-mile battle line between Leyte and Hibusan Island, where the Surigao Strait enters Leyte Gulf. Two destroyer divisions were sent down the strait to launch torpedo attacks, a third was in readiness as a follow-up, and a fourth attended the battle line. Since there were no radar-equipped aircraft available for night reconnaissance, 39 torpedo boats patrolled the strait, with orders to report any contact with the enemy and then attack.

The first contact was reported at 2230 hours, but none of the subsequent PT boat attacks managed to do any damage. At 0300 hours on 25 October the destroyer divisions began their attacks. The Japanese were sailing in a straight line with the destroyers *Michishio*, *Asagumo*, *Shigure*, and *Yamagumo* in front, followed by *Yamashiro*, *Fuso*, and *Mogami*. The *Fuso* was hit first, dropped out of line, and began to burn and explode. The *Yamashiro* was hit twice, and all the destroyers except *Shigure* were sunk or disabled. None of the American destroyers were damaged. Nishimura, now left with only three ships – *Yamashiro*, *Mogami*, and *Shigure*, plowed straight ahead toward his objective, neither ordering evasive action nor taking any notice of his damaged ships.

The formidable American battle line (three heavy and two light cruisers on the left, one heavy and two light cruisers on the right, and six battleships with a destroyer screen in the center) stretched across the mouth of the Strait; and as the three Japanese ships approached, Oldendorf found himself in the same position as if he were crossing the Japanese T. In other words, he could turn his ships at right angles to the approaching enemy and rake them with devastating broadsides, to which the Japanese could only reply with the forward guns. The American line opened fire at 0351 hours. *California*, *Tennessee*, and *West Virginia*, who were equipped with the new Mark 8 fire control radar, scored most of the hits. The other battleships, with the old Mark 3 radar, had trouble finding targets. In 18 minutes the American ships fired almost 300 rounds of 14in and 16in shells. The Japanese ships died slowly, and their commanders bravely carried on

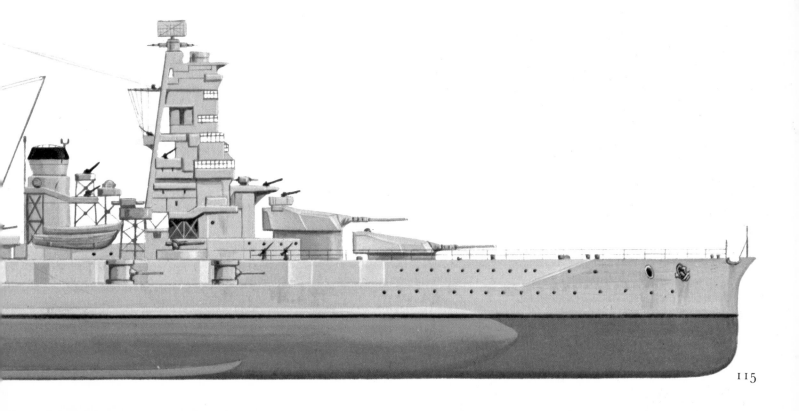

Right: The carrier battle
off Cape Engano.

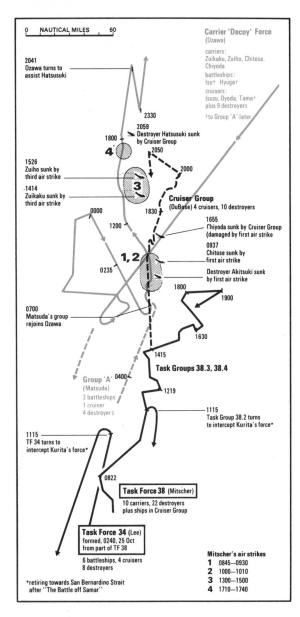

while their ships were blasted from beneath them.

At 0355 hours, *Mogami*, burning fiercely but still firing and launching torpedoes, reversed course and began to move south; just after 0400 hours her bridge was shelled, killing the commander and his staff and bringing the ship to a halt. By this time, *Yamashiro*, who had also turned south, was burning brightly against the night sky. As the American battleships moved in for the kill, two torpedos from the destroyer *Newcombe* hit and the old battleship quickly sank with Nishimura and most of the crew aboard.

Admiral Shima, following with the Second Striking Force, had intercepted messages from Nishimura as early as midnight that warned him he was in for a fight. At 0300 hours he

turned north into the strait, already able to see flashes of gunfire from the battle ahead. An American PT boat patrolling the channel knocked the light cruiser *Abakuma* out of formation with a torpedo. Undaunted, Shima carried on. Half an hour later he passed the burning *Fuso* which had broken in half. He took the two hulks, which were silhouetted by their own flames, to be two ships – the *Fuso* and the *Yamashiro* – and his fears increased. Next he came upon the *Shigure*, heading south, and then *Mogami*, apparently dead in the water. The radar showed a group of American ships some six to eight miles north of *Mogami*. Shimu ordered an attack and the *Nachi* and *Ashigara* swung over. But *Mogami* was not standing still – she was actually creeping south at about eight knots, being desperately navigated from her engine room. *Ashigara* managed to avoid a collision but the flagship *Nachi*, in the lead, collided with the *Mogami* and tore a hole in her own bow. Meanwhile Shima's four destroyers had failed to make contact with the Americans. Shima decided that to continue north would be folly, and just before 0500 hours the entire force, including the crippled *Mogami*, began to withdraw. As dawn appeared Oldendorf began a general pursuit down the strait with nearly a score of cruisers and destroyers. The *Mogami* and the destroyer *Asagumo* were sunk; the *Abakuma* went down the following day. Protection of the Leyte beach-head was still the Seventh Fleet's primary concern, however, and Oldendorf decided to break off the pursuit. Shima's remaining two heavy cruisers and two destroyers made it to safety as did *Shigure*, the only survivor of Nishima's force.

While the Battle of the Surigao Strait was going on, Admiral Kurita was cautiously working his way down the 150-mile length of the San Bernardino Strait. His crews were at battle stations, the lookouts tensely straining their eyes for the first sign of the enemy – but no enemy appeared. Halsey, who believed Kurita to be in retreat, had come to the conclusion that Center Force was no longer a serious threat. He had then taken the entire Third Fleet north to chase Ozawa's decoy force, without alerting Kinkaid to Kurita's presence or leaving a single ship to patrol the San Bernardino Strait. Both Kinkaid and Nimitz, however, believed that Halsey had left a force of heavy ships to block the entrance to Leyte Gulf.

They were soon to learn otherwise. At sunrise on 25 October Kurita emerged from the strait and discovered a group of carriers dead ahead. At 0648 hours, thinking he had stumbled across Mitscher's Task Force 38, he opened fire. The crews of what was actually an escort carrier group code named Taffy 3, under the command of Rear Admiral Sprague, were taken completely by surprise as they ate breakfast on what was to have been another routine day.

Taffy 3 was one of three elements, or units, in Rear Admiral Thomas Sprague's Task Group 77.4. Each unit consisted of four to six escort carriers or CVEs, three destroyers, and four lightly armored destroyer-escorts. Until now they had been flying routine support missions for the Leyte landings. Each carrier normally had a complement of 18 Wildcats and 12 Avengers.

They were vulnerable targets: small, slow, unarmored, and lightly gunned craft. If the handsome big carriers got most of the glory, the little escort carriers handled more of the tedious, day-to-day routine. Often called 'jeep carriers' or 'baby flattops,' they had many other names as well – of which 'bucket of bolts' is the most polite. Many crewmen insisted that CVE really stood for 'Combustible, Vulnerable, Expendable,' and indeed the little carriers were never designed for a stand-up fight.

As the shells began to splash around his ships, Sprague, a former carrier commander in the Battle of the Philippine Sea, launched whatever planes he had on board. Then the group sped off at the maximum CVE speed, sending out urgent, plain-language calls for help. Taffys 1 and 2, more than 130 miles away, launched their own planes in support. Kinkaid, who up until that time had believed the Third Fleet was covering the San Bernardino Strait, could not help – the Seventh Fleet had yet to refill its ammunition lockers after the Battle in the Surigao Strait. Halsey was much too far away to do any good; although he ordered planes from Admiral McCain's task force to assist, it would be hours before they would arrive. Taffy 3 was on its own.

The Japanese made their first mistake when, in the excitement of the moment, they believed they were seeing carriers instead of escort car-

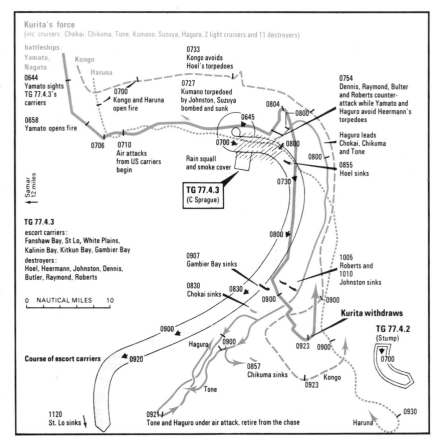

riers, cruisers instead of destroyers, and destroyers instead of destroyer escorts. The second mistake came when Kurita, instead of forming a battle line with his heavy ships and sending his destroyers in for torpedo attacks, ordered General Attack. This meant every ship for itself, and threw the Japanese force into total confusion.

Sprague, faced with 'the ultimate in desperate circumstances,' formed his carriers in a rough circle surrounded by the destroyers and destroyer escorts. As the Japanese ships closed in 'with disconcerting rapidity,' he ordered a

Top: The battle off Samar.

Above:
Crew on board the sinking carrier *Zuikaku* cheer as they go down. There was such a shortage of pilots by October 1944 that the only role assigned the carriers in the battle was as a decoy force.

torpedo attack to divert them and turned the carriers south-southwest to get nearer Leyte.

Although they had twice the speed, the Japanese ships were unable to close in on the escort carriers, for the tenacious defense put up by Taffy 3's planes and destroyers forced them into constant evasive action. Both planes and destroyers attacked over and over again until their ammunition was gone – and then made dry runs to divert Japanese fire from the carriers.

The bombers managed to put one heavy cruiser, *Suzuya*, out of commission early in the battle, and later sank two other cruisers. One of the destroyers, the *Johnston*, forced the heavy cruiser *Kumano* out of the fighting before being hit herself by three 14-inch and three 6-inch shells. Even when her power was gone and her engine room out she continued to fight, firing her guns manually, until three cruisers came up and blasted her until she had to be abandoned. Meanwhile the other two destroyers, *Hoel* and *Heermann*, carried on the battle. *Hoel* finally sank, having been hit 40 times.

Despite the efforts of their defenders, the American carriers were taking a pounding; the *Gambier Bay* was sunk at 0907 hours, and the *Kalinin Bay* took 13 hits from 8-inch guns. Then at 1230 hours Kurita broke off the action and began to retire; not realizing the damage his cruisers were beginning to inflict on the carriers, he had decided to reassemble his force and make another attempt to get into Leyte Gulf. Just then he learned of Southern Force's defeat in the Surigao Strait. As he turned away, 70 Avengers and Wildcats from Taffy 2 and 3 arrived and a signalman on the bridge of Sprague's flagship shouted 'Goddammit, boys, they're getting away.'

Getting away they were, and just in time – Oldendorf's battleships were waiting for them at the mouth of Leyte Gulf, while both Task Force 38 and land-based planes were being prepared for a massive air attack. Had he not turned back, Kurita would have shared Nishimura's fate. As it was, the most powerful force Japan had been able to amass since Midway had been turned back by a small, weak, relatively defenseless, but determined squadron – demonstrating the vulnerability of capital ships without air cover.

But the Taffys' troubles were not yet over. On 25 October Taffy 1 became the first American force to endure a kamikaze attack ('Divine Wind'), and later the same day Taffy 3 was attacked eight times and the *St Lo* was sunk. The kamikaze were a special air corps, organized in a last desperate attempt to make up for Japan's rapidly dwindling air power. It had become nearly impossible for a bomber to score a hit on a ship since the invention of the proximity armed fuze for anti-aircraft shells, but the sacrificial crashing of a plane into an enemy ship would have the same effect by detonating the bombs on board and setting the fuel on fire. In addition, obsolete planes and untrained pilots could be used. Vice-Admiral Onishi of First Air Fleet had already begun training a kamikaze corps when Rear Admiral Arima attempted the first deliberate kamikaze attack against the carrier *Franklin* on 15 October, and thousands of young Japanese volunteered to sacrifice their lives for the Emperor.

Meanwhile, Halsey and the powerful Third Fleet, who had been assigned to 'cover and support' the Army and to 'destroy enemy naval and air forces in or threatening the Philippines' were somewhere off Cape Engano. Although the first duty of a covering force in an amphibious operation is to protect the landing force, Halsey saw his primary objective as the destruction of the Japanese fleet – and indeed his orders (which he had helped draft) gave him this option.

The Northern Force under Admiral Ozawa had left the Inland Sea on schedule, taking a course that would allow them to be seen – but not too soon. Ozawa had one heavy carrier and three light carriers with a total of only 116 planes between them, two 'hermaphrodite' carriers (battleships with cut-down superstructures to make room for a short flight deck), and a screen of three light cruisers and nine destroyers. On the morning of 24 October search planes discovered part of Task Force 38, and Ozawa sent out 76 planes to attack it. Only 29 returned. Finally, at 1540 hours, American search planes located the Japanese carrier force; the report, however, did not reach Halsey until 1700 hours.

Hearing of the sighting, the aggressive Halsey was galvanized into action – and into a critical error of judgment. Dismissing Kurita's force from his mind he ordered all 64 ships and 787 planes of the Third Fleet in pursuit of Ozawa's 17 ships and 116 planes.

At 0430 hours on the morning of 25 October Halsey launched his planes against the Japanese, who were reported to be 200 miles off Cape Engano on Luzon. The first strike came in at 0800 hours – first the Helldivers, then the strafing Wildcats, and finally the Avengers sweeping in to release their torpedoes from 700–1000ft at ranges of 1400–1600yds. Three more major strikes followed in quick succession. Without a Combat Air Patrol, Ozawa was forced to rely on evasive tactics and anti-aircraft fire – perhaps the most deadly barrage produced by either side during the war. Nevertheless, all four carriers and a destroyer went down during these strikes.

Halsey began getting calls for help from Taffy 3 at 0820 hours, but made no real move to send assistance; he wanted to keep his entire battle force with him to clean up the Japanese 'cripples' after the air strikes and to chase the two battleship carriers. He changed his mind, however, around 1000 hours when even Nimitz began asking what he was doing and what provisions had been made to guard the San Bernardino Strait. At 1055 hours he sent one carrier group and most of the battle line south – much too late to be of any real help.

The remaining cruisers and destroyers followed Northern Force, finishing off a light cruiser and a large destroyer; but one light cruiser, the two battleship carriers, and five destroyers managed to escape. Ozawa, who was considered the ablest Japanese admiral after Yamamoto, had managed to save both Center Force and Northern Force from annihilation, despite the fact that he had 'expected complete destruction' on the mission. Halsey, on the other hand, had piled error upon error. The first, of course, was rising to the bait at all. The second was failing to leave a strong force to block the strait or at least to tell Kinkaid that it was unguarded. The third was his failure to retain a sufficient force to complete the destruction of Ozawa's force at the very end.

By 26 October the battle was over. The Allies had lost a light carrier, two escort carriers, two destroyers, and a destroyer escort. The Japanese were down three battleships, one heavy carrier, three light carriers, six heavy cruisers, four light cruisers, and nine destroyers. The two high points of the battle were Oldendorf's disposition of the Seventh Fleet in the night battle in the Surigao Strait and Ozawa's execution of his decoy mission. The low points were the Allies' failure to destroy either Center Force or Northern Force, and Kurita's failure to sink all of Taffy 3, which he might have done had he been able to retain tactical control of his force.

The greatest weakness on the American side was the divided command at the top. If one commander, whether MacArthur or Nimitz, had been in overall control, Halsey could not have decamped as he did without asking permission.

There are many reasons for the Japanese defeat: the overwhelming complexity of *Sho-1*; bad co-ordination between commanders; their inability, despite their bravery and competence, to alter their tactics to suit the circumstances; and perhaps most important, the lack of air power. If Leyte Gulf holds one great lesson, it is the helplessness of a modern fleet without air cover.

Leyte Gulf was the last main fleet action in history – and in view of the revolutionary changes in naval warfare, is likely to remain so. It is perhaps fitting then that it was also the last engagement of a battle line, a tactical device for naval combat that dates from the reign of James I and that was first used successfully in the Battle of Lowestoft in 1655. As Oldendorf crossed the T at the mouth of Surigao Strait the battle line went into oblivion along with the Greek phalanx, the galleys of Salamis, the Spanish pikeman, and the English longbow.

Although battleship tactics began to change early in the twentieth century with the development of the mine, torpedo, and submarine, the battleship itself remained the backbone of every navy until well into World War II. Between 1939 and 1945, however, the carrier came into its own; and by the Battle of Midway, as we have seen, it had become the dominant factor in naval warfare. For the rest of the war, battleships – at least in the American navy – were assigned support roles for carriers and amphibious landings. During the postwar period the major navies ceased building battleships altogether.

Today another technological revolution – the development of the atomic submarine and its associated, sophisticated weaponry – might well mean that the carrier is well on the way to assuming an auxiliary role with the battleship.

Marines of the 5th Marine
Division crawl their way onto
Iwo Jima. Twenty minutes
after the first Marines landed
the Japanese opened up and
pinned them down to the
beaches.

7 IWO JIMA
The Island Fortress

Iwo Jima is an island in the Bonin chain and is only four and a half miles long, and two and a quarter miles wide. It is nestled at the southern end of the chain which extends due south for 700 miles from the coast of Japan. The entire island is flat except for the rocky promontory of Mount Suribachi, an extinct volcano, which is 556 feet high on the southern portion of the island.

Iwo Jima was of great importance to the Japanese who used it for staging purposes on their routes to the central and southern Pacific. The early years of the war saw them build two airfields on it and after the fall of the Marshall Islands their importance grew. The conquest of the Marianas by the United States in July 1944 and their subsequent utilization for air attacks against the homeland even further

enhanced the importance of Iwo Jima. It was more than evident that the Americans would need it for a staging point and advanced air base for the ultimate invasion of Japan.

The Japanese realized this and in early 1944 dispatched the 109th Division to the island. This unit was commanded by Lieutenant General Kuribayashi. He immediately strengthened all defenses, and began work on a third airfield in the north. Kuribayashi knew that the beaches could not be held and so he based his entire defensive strategy on a do-or-die effort around Mount Suribachi and the Motoyama plateau. The US constantly bombarded the island but nonetheless, defensive positions were built in depth between No 1 and No 2 airfields, and between No 2 airfield and Motoyama, connected by a very intricate net-

Above: Douglas SBD-4 Dauntlesses and Grumman F6F Hellcats on board the USS *Essex*.

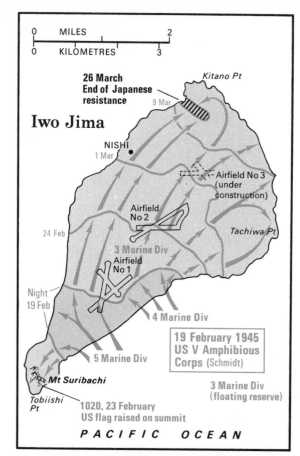

Iwo Jima

MILES 0 — 2
KILOMETRES 0 — 3

26 March
End of Japanese
resistance

Kitano Pt

9 Mar

NISHI
1 Mar

Airfield No 3
(under construction)

Airfield
No 2

24 Feb

Tachiwa Pt

3 Marine Div
Airfield
No 1

Night
19 Feb

4 Marine Div

5 Marine Div

**19 February 1945
US V Amphibious
Corps** (Schmidt)

3 Marine Div
(floating reserve)

Mt Suribachi

Tobiishi
Pt

1020, 23 February
US flag raised on summit

PACIFIC OCEAN

Below: Armorers of the 45th Fighter Squadron, 15th Fighter Group, based on Saipan load ammunition onto a North American P-51 Mustang. The Mustang was being prepared for a raid on Iwo Jima to soften up its defenses. These raids did not in fact achieve much because the Japanese had dug their defensive positions underground.

work of tunnels. These defenses were supported by heavy artillery and mortars conveniently situated in caves and camouflaged concrete emplacements. The same type of defenses were built around Mount Suribachi and, in addition, the beaches were heavily mined. By January 1945 the Iwo Jima garrison was over 21,000 strong and was waiting for the first Marines to land.

The reasoning behind the American decision to take the island was dictated by their policy of strategically bombing Japan into submission. As the Japanese High Command had realized high losses of B-29 bombers on missions over Japan meant that the US had to ensure better fighter protection for bombers. The B-29s had been flying unescorted because none of the American fighters had the range to make the 2800-mile round trip between the Marianas and Japan. Iwo Jima was an excellent choice as an air base because it was only 660 nautical miles from Tokyo and it had already been developed by the Japanese for that purpose. In fact aircraft on Iwo Jima were used to bomb the Marianas and it was necessary to knock it out as an airbase. The other calculation the American planners made was that since Iwo Jima was traditionally Japanese territory, its loss would be a psychological blow to the Japanese people.

With all these considerations in mind planning for the operation to take Iwo Jima had been initiated in September 1943. Following the fall of the Marianas Admiral Nimitz placed the entire operation in the capable hands of Admiral Raymond Spruance and his 5th Fleet. The man in charge of the actual Joint Expeditionary Force was Rear Admiral Kelly Turner. Rear Admiral Marc Mitscher's fast carrier force was given the task of covering the main force. Spruance knew all about the heavy Japanese preparations so he arranged for the 7th USAAF to attack the island's defenses with B-24s from the Marianas. This continuous bombardment was to start on 31 January and continue until 15 February. Then a three-day naval bombardment was to begin. To create a diversion to pull away any Japanese air support for the island, Spruance ordered the complete complement of the fast carrier force to attack targets in the Tokyo area and airfields for the first time on 16 and 17 February.

Consolidated B-24 Liberators drop 55-gallon drum incendiary bombs on a wooded area near the area planned for the first wave of the invasion force on Iwo Jima. On that day, 1 February 1945, 21 bombers dropped eight drums each.

The USS *Nevada* bombards coastal positions on 19 February 1945 prior to the invasion of Iwo Jima.

Inset: North American P-51 Mustang returning from a bombing raid on Iwo Jima.

The ground operations were placed in the hands of Lieutenant General Holland 'Howlin' Mad' Smith, who had been the commander of the operations in the Gilberts, Marshalls and Marianas. The invasion itself would be undertaken by Major General Harry Schmidt's V Amphibious Corps, which had amassed as much experience as Holland Smith of amphibious techniques. The V Amphibious Corps consisted of three divisions: the 3rd Marine Division, led by Major General Erskine; the 4th Marine Division, led by Major General Cates; the 5th Marine Division, led by Major General Rockey, which was a new unit composed of 40 percent veterans.

The Amphibious Support Force arrived off Iwo Jima on 16 February and proceeded to soften the Japanese defenses. The Japanese, who had long expected the invasion, were convinced this was the main landing and opened fire with their heaviest artillery at 1100. The US had sent out frogmen to reconnoiter the shore emplacements and these men suffered over 170 casualties but they were able to bring

back detailed reports on the Japanese defenses. Prior to D-Day these concealed coastal guns were extensively shelled by the US Navy.

On the morning of 19 February Turner arrived with the main force, some 450 vessels of the 5th Fleet. Directly after dawn the most concentrated pre-landing bombardment of the war was initiated by seven battleships, seven cruisers and numerous destroyers against shore defenses. During this bombardment over 31,000 shells were fired, and in addition, the the fast carrier force strafed the beaches, known

defensive positions and camouflaged artillery for over 25 minutes. The first Marines were landing on the southeastern beaches by 0900 hours. Although the naval and air bombardments had been tremendous, the damage to defensive works had been minimal. Once the initial landings were accomplished the Japanese garrison erupted from their hidden caves and underground shelters, and the Marines were immediately pinned down on the beaches. The weather, always a variable factor in amphibious landings, changed for the worse.

Right: The US Navy's most
important duty was to
neutralize the defenses of
the outlying islands. Here
the 40mm guns of a battleship
shell the island of Ie Shima.

Below: Mount Suribachi as seen
from the invasion fleet on D-Day.

One of the first pictures to be taken of Marines going ashore on Iwo Jima on 19 February 1945.

Rising surf and extremely strong currents delayed landing reinforcements, tanks and stores of equipment. The Marines were hard pressed but undaunted – as usual they plowed ahead.

The Japanese plan had been to wait for the Marines to get ashore and then open up. But 20 minutes after the initial landings when they had launched their artillery and mortars it was already too late as the Marines had brought ashore all the equipment they needed.

One specific action earned Sergeant Darrell Cole the Medal of Honor for conspicuous gallantry above and beyond the call of duty. While acting as leader of a machine-gun section of B Company, First Battalion, 23rd Marines, 4th Marine Division, Sergeant Cole was advancing with one squad of his section in the initial assault wave under heavy small arms, mortar and artillery fire, up the sloping beach toward No 1 airfield when he personally, at an

extremely high risk to himself, destroyed two hostile emplacements which were endangering his unit's progress with hand grenades. Continuing to advance they were brought under tremendous enemy fire which succeeded in bringing their advance to a halt. Sergeant Cole set up one of his machine guns and managed to eliminate one of the enemy pillboxes which had his men pinned down. He quickly made an on-the-spot tactical judgment and armed only with a pistol and one hand grenade, advanced alone against the remaining two enemy pillboxes. He threw his hand grenade into the enemy pillbox, and returned for another grenade. He ran withering machine-gun fire from the enemy not once but three times before he succeeded in destroying all of the enemy positions. For this superb action under constant enemy fire, he was awarded the highest honor that a grateful country can bestow upon a hero.

One of the many heavily fortified Japanese pillboxes on Iwo. As they advanced the Marines discovered how well dug in the enemy had been.

Lieutenant General Holland Smith and Major General Harry Schmidt stand in front of the command post of the V Amphibious Corps on Iwo Jima.

With his bayonet fixed at charge, this Marine died trying to claw his way across the beach on the first day of the invasion.

He was only one of 22 Medal-of-Honor winners at Iwo Jima.

By the evening of 19 February 30,000 Marines had been landed but the casualty rate was extremely high, more than 3000 dead. The Marines had eked out a beach-head only 1000 yards deep at the edge of No 1 airfield, and on the next day reached the west coast at the foot of Mount Suribachi. For the next three days the Marines fought to gain control of Mount Suribachi and finally at 1020 on 23 February a 40-man patrol was able to raise the Stars and Stripes on the summit. This feat was recorded in some of the most famous photographs of World War II.

Above: Members of the 5th Marine Division work their way inch by inch from Red Beach Number One toward Suribachi Yama.

Left: The 2nd Battalion, 27th Marines faces intense fire as they try to move forward.

Left: The scene on the beach on the first day. Some Marines never made it past the beach and died in the soft volcanic ash.

137

Spruance's 5th Fleet was not left unmarked during the battle. On the night of 20/21 February 20 Japanese aircraft hit Mitscher's fast carrier force without inflicting much damage but the next day, the *Saratoga* was hit by five kamikazes, causing substantial damage. Only two hours later, another five attacked her but only one succeeded in reaching the ship. This time the damage was so extensive that the grand old lady had to return to the west coast for major repairs. On that same evening two more kamikazes attacked the escort carrier *Bismarck Sea* and within a couple of hours that ship went down. A reprisal raid against Japan was launched from the fast carrier force on 25 February but they were for the most part ineffective; immediately afterward bad weather set in. Mitscher then withdrew to his base at Ulithi. He did manage to make one parting strike against Okinawa on his way back.

On Iwo Jima the 4th and 5th Marine Division were fighting to gain control of the two northernmost airfields and on 25 February the 3rd Marine Division was brought in. The advance had stopped as the Marines had become enmeshed in the elaborate defensive network, built by the Japanese. Artillery could not get at the underground positions and tanks could not negotiate the terrain. In fact Japanese and US casualty figures were evenly matched: it was merely a question of when the last Japanese would be killed. The final breakthrough did not come until 9 March when elements of the 3rd Marines reached the northeast shore of the island. The Japanese were finally isolated in a pocket near Kitano point and it was just a question of mopping up resistance. The Marines discovered the underground bunkers and caves which had protected the Japanese so well.

Left: The official flag-raising ceremony which took place on 14 March 1945, once the southern portion of the island had been secured.

Left: A young Korean bids goodbye to his friends and family as he sets out on a mission in mid-1944. In the first stages of the war Koreans and Formosans, though under Japanese colonial rule, were not allowed to join the Japanese forces. By 1943, however, lack of manpower obliged Japan to accept them, and many fought heroically.

Right: Triumphant Marines of the 5th Division pose with a captured Japanese flag.

Center right: The final push: an observer pinpoints a machine-gun nest on a map and relays the information to artillery so that it can be eliminated.

By 6 March P-51 Mustangs of the 7th USAAF were using the airfields on Iwo Jima and by April they were escorting B-29s to Japan. On 26 March 300 Japanese launched a final suicidal attack and Iwo Jima was finally under US control. It had been the most costly Pacific battle to date. Of the 23,000-man garrison defending the island only 1083 were taken prisoner. US casualties totaled 6812 killed and 19,189 wounded – almost 30 percent of the landing force. The Allied planners had underestimated the number of defenders on the island and had anticipated an easy operation. It turned out to be one of the most brutal operations of the war. With all the advantages the US had gained with control of the sea and superior air power, yet again the Japanese had proved an unpredictable opponent. The final tragedy was that Iwo Jima became just an emergency landing base for B-29s. Therefore the long and bitter struggle for Iwo Jima proved to be, to some extent, a useless exercise.

Below: Two Marines blast their way through the Japanese defenses using flame throwers.

Below right: Marine wiremen repair telephone lines toward the front lines and ensure adequate communication.

Center left: Two Marines remain on guard in case the smoke conceals hidden snipers.

Left: An artillery unit fires rockets against specific targets on Iwo.

Below: Lieutenant General Yoshio Tachibana of the Japanese Army signs the final surrender of the Bonin Islands on 3 September 1945.

The USS *New Mexico* bombards Okinawa prior to the invasion.

8 OKINAWA
The Last Hurdle

In 1943 at the Sextant Conference in Cairo a timetable was established for Admiral Nimitz's Central Pacific approach to Japan. Until October 1944 the primary target following the operations on the Marianas was Formosa. Operation Causeway, the amphibious assault on Formosa, was planned to follow General Douglas MacArthur's recapture of the Philippines. Although plans for Causeway were well advanced, in view of the staff and service shortages, the Joint Chiefs of Staff agreed to ignore Formosa and attack Iwo Jima and Okinawa.

Thus Operation Iceberg was born and Nimitz's staff began preparing detailed plans for the operation. Okinawa's strategic importance lay in its location. The island was the most heavily defended of the Ryukyu Islands and it was only 330 nautical miles from Formosa and 350 nautical miles from Kyushu, Japan. Once captured it would make an excellent airbase to step up the bombing of Japan. Okinawa could be used to train troops for the final assault on Japan and it also had the only two fleet anchorages available between Formosa and Kyushu.

Following the defeat at the Battle of Leyte Gulf the Japanese High Command was only too aware that the last battle was approaching. It was agreed that the final battle would be fought in Japan but also that the Ryukyus' defenses would be strengthened to delay the US invasion. After April 1944 Okinawa became a top priority for the Japanese and in August 1944 Lieutenant General Mitsuri Ushijima arrived to take charge of operations. Major General Isamu Cho was assigned to him and together they made a formidable team. Between June and August units from China, Manchuria and Japan were sent to Okinawa. These troops were in the main well trained but inexperienced and Cho, with his belief in iron discipline, prepared them for battle. The 9th Infantry Division had provided the backbone of the Okinawan defenses but the Japanese High Command decided to transfer them in December 1944 to the Philippines. They never made it to Luzon because of US control of the seas and spent the rest of the war in Formosa. Ushijima lost his best division which was never replaced; however he did receive massive supplies of ammunition and artillery. His defense force consisted of the 24th, 28th and 62nd

Division, and the 44th Independent Mixed Division. By the time of the US invasion he had a force of 80,000 men, and of these 20,000 were native Okinawans. Ushijima decided early on that the doctrine of attack had been ineffective in earlier operations and since his brief was to obtain the maximum delay he decided against attacking the US on the beaches and instead withdrew to the south, where he had a massive defense network built in the hills. The new slogan for the Japanese was 'One plane for one warship. One boat for one ship. One man for ten enemy. One man for one tank.'

The US assault on Okinawa had been planned for 1 March 1945 but it had to be postponed for a month because the operation on Iwo Jima had taken longer than planned. The US had assembled a force which was more than experienced. Although the Tenth Army as such had not taken part in any operations before its units were veterans of campaigns throughout the Pacific. The commander of the Tenth Army was General Simon Bolivar Buckner, whose previous command had been in Alaska. The Tenth Army comprised the III Amphibious Corps, under Major General Roy Geiger, and the XXIV Corps, under Major General Courtney Hodges. The III Amphibious Corps was composed of the 1st and 6th Marine Divisions, which included men who had fought on Guadalcanal, New Georgia, Bougainville, Guam and Peleliu. The XXIV Corps was composed of the 7th Infantry Division and the 96th Infantry Division, whose units had fought in the Gilberts, Marshalls, Marianas and in the Philippines. Despite the fact that some of the men had been fighting for 30 months in the Pacific, all units underwent extensive training programs for the operations.

While the ground forces were engaged in training, Buckner's staff grappled with the logistical problems. The logistical plan for Okinawa was 'the most elaborate one of its kind developed during World War II, involving prearranged movement of both assault and cargo shipping over vast ocean distances.' The Naval Assault Force was similar to the one utilized against Iwo Jima. Vice-Admiral Raymond Spruance was in charge of the entire operation; Vice-Admiral Marc Mitscher commanded the fast carrier force; Vice-Admiral Richmond Kelly Turner commanded the

Above: Lieutenant Simon Bolivar Buckner (left), commander of ground forces on Okinawa, and Vice-Admiral Richmond Kelly Turner, commander of the naval forces.

Left: Major General Lemuel Shepherd was the Commander of the 6th Marine Division.

Above: A US cruiser fires its guns off Okinawa in April 1945.

Right: An anti-aircraft unit in action on a battleship off Okinawa.

Joint Expeditionary Force. There were numerous support groups: the Demonstration Group, commanded by Rear Admiral Jerrauld Wright, carried 2nd Marine Division; the Western Islands Attack Group, commanded by Rear Admiral Ingolf Kiland, carried the 77th Infantry Division; the Floating Reserve Group, commanded by Commodore McGovern, carried the 27th Infantry Group. The British Pacific Fleet also took part in the operation, under the command of Vice-Admiral Sir Bernard Rawlings. It comprised the battleships *King George V* and *Howe,* carriers *Indomitable, Victorious, Indefatigable* and *Illustrious,* the cruisers *Swiftsure, Black Prince, Argonaut, Euryalus* and *Gambia,* and 11 destroyers. The entire armada totaled 1450 ships of various types. The US plan was to take Kerama Retto on 26 March 1945 so that the naval units could have a protected anchorage for refueling and resupplying. The III Amphibious Corps was to land north of Hagushi on Okinawa and the XXIV Corps south so that they could seize the Yontan and Kadena airfields.

From February onward US naval and aerial forces subjected Okinawa to intense bombardments. The Japanese responded by stepping up their kamikaze attacks so that by the time of the invasion there were very few aircraft left on Okinawa. The kamikaze attacks were aimed at knocking out the US carriers so that the aircraft from Kyushu and Sakishima Gunto could be used to defend Okinawa. Between 26–31 March some six US ships, including Spruance's flagship *Indianapolis* were put out of commission and at least ten other ships suffered much damage from kamikaze attacks. Nonetheless on 18 and 19 March the fast carrier force had attacked airfields in Kyushu and shipping in the Inland Sea as a preliminary 'softening up' process. The XXI Bomber Command in the Marianas was ordered to attack selected targets and various airfields in Kyushu between the 27–31 March, and in addition to mine the Shimonoseki Strait, the narrows between Kyushu and the main island of Honshu, through which the bulk of all Japanese shipping sailed.

Above: LSMRs bombarding
Okinawa before the Okinawa
invasion.

Right: The 6th Marine
Division presses forward.

Left: For the first time in the war in the Far East Japanese troops surrendered in large numbers.

Left: Marines search for snipers in the ruins of the city of Naha, the capital of Okinawa.

Center left: Two Marines armed with a bazooka inch their way up a hill, two miles north of Naha.

Prior to the main landing on Okinawa the 77th Division landed on Kerama Retto on 26 March. Minesweepers moved in to clear that island and others in the Ryukyus of mines. An intense aerial and naval bombardment preceded the landing on Kerama. On 26 March at 0801 the first of four assault battalions hit their targets on the islands. By the end of the day units of the 77th Division controlled three islands and had established a foothold on two others. In fact shortly after the first landings the US troops had uncovered and destroyed

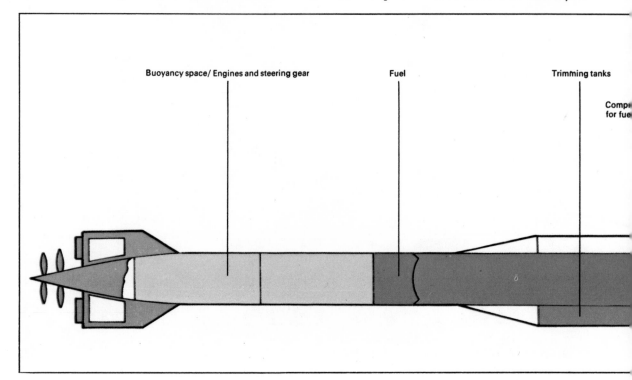

Buoyancy space/ Engines and steering gear   Fuel   Trimming tanks   Comp for fue

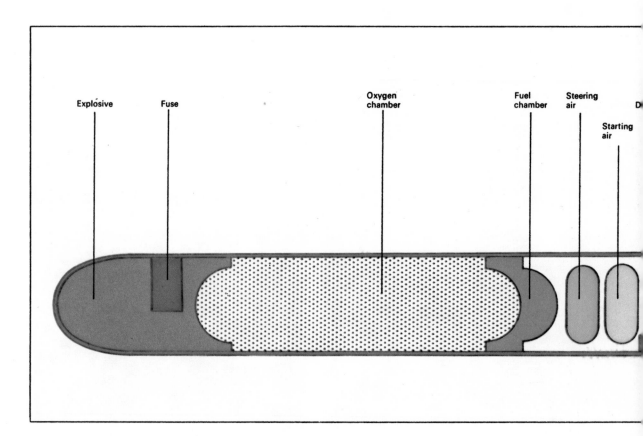

Explosive   Fuse   Oxygen chamber   Fuel chamber   Steering air   D

Starting air

more than 350 enemy suicide boats which would have been used against the main invasion force on Okinawa. Although Japanese troops were still resisting on 31 March the US forces had gained control of Kerama Retto for the loss of 31 men killed and another 81 injured.

The date chosen for the main assault on Okinawa was not only April Fool's Day it was also Easter Sunday. Under a blistering naval bombardment, an unopposed amphibious landing was accomplished on the Hagushi beach.

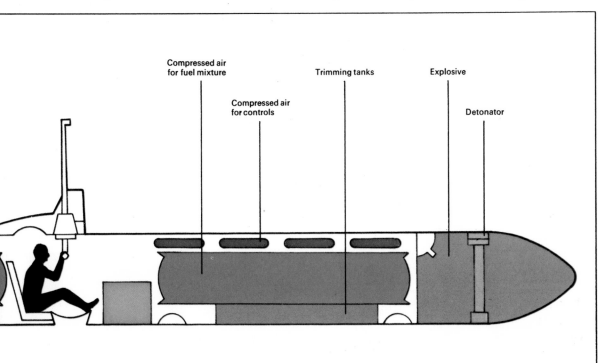

Compressed air for fuel mixture

Compressed air for controls

Trimming tanks

Explosive

Detonator

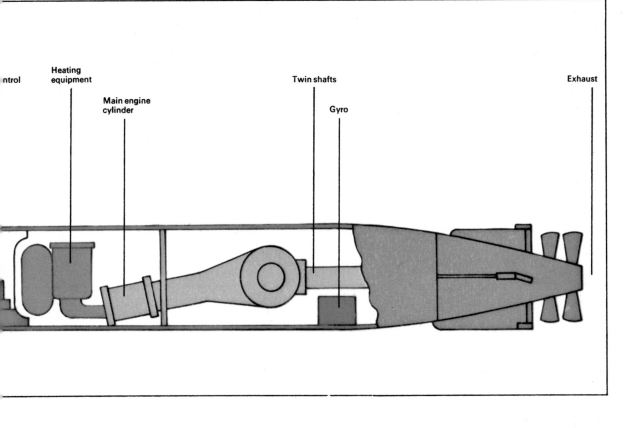

Heating equipment

Main engine cylinder

Twin shafts

Gyro

Exhaust

Left: The *Kaiten* human torpedo was built as a suicide weapon in Japan's last desperate attempt to defend the home islands. They were based on the Type 93 long-lance torpedo.

Below left: The long-lance torpedo was 24 inches in diameter and was the most advanced project developed by the Imperial Navy. Its liquid oxygen motor drove it at a speed of 49 knots.

Above: A Marine stands in
the wreckage of a theater
building in Naha.

Right: Elements of the 6th
Marine Division make their
way to the front line on the
outskirts of Naha.

Opposition was slight, and by early evening both Yontan and Kadena airfields were secured. Everything was 'looking good' and by 6 April the Tenth Army held the center of the island and could now pivot in either direction. The Marine Divisions had reached Nago at the base of the Motobu Peninsula, and both captured airfields were back in use. The first 72 hours of the invasion saw the Japanese 8th Air Division launch in excess of 80 aircraft to attack Allied shipping off Okinawa. The results were good: one destroyer, an escort carrier, two LSTs, one LCT sunk, two transports badly damaged, and another six vessels receiving minor damage.

The Japanese Combined Fleet commanded by Admiral Toyoda ordered a naval force consisting of the battleship *Yamato* under Vice-Admiral Ito, the light cruiser *Yahagi* and eight destroyers to sail from the Inland Sea and engage Allied shipping off Okinawa on 8 April. This final act of bravado on the part of the Imperial Navy was very reminiscent of the sinking of the *Prince of Wales* and *Repulse* because they too had lacked air cover. This force was sighted by a US submarine which relayed the important information to Mitscher. His aircraft located the enemy at 0822 hours on 7 April, 85 miles west of Kyushu. Two hundred and ninety-six aircraft were in the air and poised for the attack at 1000 hours. Meanwhile, Turner had placed a strong force of battleships, cruisers and destroyers across the eventual path of the enemy force just in case it managed to elude or survive the massive air attack which was in process. By 1430 hours the power of the Imperial Navy in the western Pacific was most definitely at an end: the *Yamato* and *Yahagi* were both sunk, and four destroyers were sunk as well. The remaining four made it back to the Inland Sea but the the end for Japan was now in sight.

Kamikaze attacks were increased on the Allied picket fleet off Okinawa. By 8 April the 6th Marine Division had secured the northern end of Okinawa and was beginning its drive into the Motobu peninsula. The Japanese were in strong defensive positions on the 1500-foot Yae Tae hills. On 14 April the Marines came down on them like hot balls of fire, driving everything before them, so that by 19 April the entire peninsula was in the hands of the US Marines.

Above: A kamikaze pilot with the rank of first lieutenant salutes after receiving the orders for his last mission.

Left: A kamikaze pilot on Kyushu before his final flight to Okinawa.

153

Above: Plane-handling
activities aboard USS *Cowpens*.
Cowpens played a crucial role
in Task Group 50.1 in 1943
and Task Group 58.4 during
the Battle of the Philippine
Sea.

Right: Landing Ship Tank
829, with its causeway lashed
to the side, approached the
Okinawa shore.

Above: Landing craft off
Okinawa on the landing day.

Left: Amtraks heading for a
beach past LSI(L) 809 at the
Okinawan landings.

155

The Marines continued to mop up the northern portion of the island until they were redeployed in May to the southern half of the island.

After clearing the northern part of Okinawa the next important target was Ie Shima, which lay northwest of the Motobu peninsula and was a large enough island to provide a useful air base. Again units of the 77th Division were used for the amphibious assault on 16 April. There was little opposition on landing but by mid-afternoon of 16 April the Japanese, concealed in caves and fortified tombs, were fighting for every inch of ground. There were more than 7000 Japanese troops on the island and they had converted Ie Shima into a fortress with an intricate maze of defenses. For six days the US fought in hand-to-hand conflict using bayonets and grenades until 21 April when resistance was finally overcome. Casualties in this operation were heavy: the Americans lost 239 killed, 879 wounded and 19 missing while the Japanese losses were 4709 killed and 149 captured. This struggle on Ie Shima would have remained unknown to the American public but for the tragic death of Ernest Pyle, the distinguished war correspondent. He died on the outskirts of Ie on 18 April.

The desperate attempts to stave off defeat on Okinawa continued. By 6 April Admiral Soemu Toyoda was ready to launch the first and largest co-ordinated kamikaze attack yet witnessed by the US troops. Fourteen planes were sent out to knock out the airfields on Okinawa but they achieved little but surface damage and did not knock out any aircraft. More than 100 fighters were then sent off to attack the fast carrier force and draw enemy fighters away from Okinawa. In all 699 planes (of which 355 were suicide sorties) were used in the attack on Okinawa between 6–7 April and they did cause much damage, including destroying all 81mm mortar ammunition. A second mass kamikaze attack was mounted on 12–13 April this time using 392 aircraft and it achieved almost the same amount of damage. Most of the aircraft were flown by inexperienced pilots and carrier-based aircraft were able to shoot them down before they reached their target. A third raid took place on 15–16 April and a fourth on 27–28 April and by this time US pilots had become expert at knocking them down.

On 9 April the XXIV Corps had come up against the Shuri defenses and since they could not make any headway General Hodges halted the advance and decided to mount an all-out offensive to knock the Japanese out with one blow. The offensive was planned for 19 April and during the four days preceding it the Japanese were subjected to intensive fire. Over 905 sorties were flown to soften up the Japanese positions. Also the firepower of six battleships, six cruisers and nine destroyers was directed against the Japanese line. The XXIV confidently expected to break through the Shuri line but soon after the attack was launched on 19 April it was apparent that the Japanese were so well dug-in that the US could make little impression. On 24 April the attack was renewed and this time made considerable ground because Ushijima had skillfully withdrawn from that line, unbeknown to the Americans. The US Army was not making the

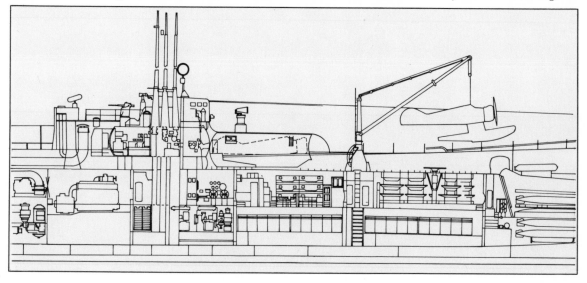

Right: The center section of the Japanese *1.58* submarine, which was launched in 1944. She was armed with six 21-inch torpedo tubes, one 5.5-inch gun and two 25-mm anti-aircraft guns.

Above: Vought F4U Corsairs
are silhouetted by anti-
aircraft tracers during a raid
by Japan-based bombers on
Yontan airfield, Okinawa.

Left: In a desperate attempt
to check the American
advance the Japanese sent
a suicide mission to destroy
Yontan airfield. Some of the
troops crashlanded on the
airstrip and managed to
destroy the two transports in
the picture. Most of the
aircraft assigned to this
mission were knocked out
before they reached the
airfield.

headway which had been expected of it and Lieutenant General Buckner redeployed the III Marine Amphibious Force, the 1st and 6th Marine Divisions, to take over the right flank from XXIV Corps which then moved over to the left flank.

Meanwhile the seemingly indestructible Japanese were suffering heavy losses and were beginning to lose ground. On 2 May at a conference at Shuri Castle the idea was mooted that it was time to mount an army-sized, all-out counterattack led by the 24th Division. Colonel Hiromichi Yahara, the operations officer of the Thirty-second Army, pointed out that the Japanese tactics had been successful up to now in that the US were suffering heavy casualties and that a counterattack was bound to fail given the numerical and material superiority of the Americans. His advice went unheeded and Ushijima decided to follow Cho's advice and mount a counterattack which took place at 0500 on 5 May. The Japanese offensive was well planned and co-ordinated with kamikaze attacks from Kyushu but failed to make any impact in the face of the intense US artillery barrage. By the evening Ushijima was forced to admit his mistake and issued an order to revert to the former tactics.

Right: Vice-Admiral Marc Mitscher on board his flagship. As commander of the fast carrier group throughout the Pacific War his role was crucial.

Above: The Martin B-26 Marauder was a medium bomber. It played a significant part in the Battle of Midway and during the early stages of the Pacific War. It continued in service until after the end of the war.

Left: The naval commanders come ashore to inspect the front lines on Okinawa. Admirals Nimitz and Spruance (wearing the sun helmet) are accompanied by army personnel.

Right: During the fighting
on the Shuri Line the seated
Marine witnessed the death
of a friend.

Buckner's reaction was to order an immediate renewal of a full-scale attack of the defenses of Shuri Castle, scheduled for 11 May. The American offensive against the Japanese line from the Asa river estuary to Yonbaru failed again and a contributing factor was the heavy rain which had turned the battle lines to mud. Wana Ridge and Sugar Loaf Hill were two of the main objectives.

One action of conspicuous gallantry earned Major Henry Courtney the Medal of Honor. Major Courtney was Executive Officer, Second Battalion, 22nd Marines, 6th Marine Division and was ordered to hold for the night of 14/15 May 1945, in static defense behind Sugar Loaf Hill after leading the advance elements of his command in a prolonged fire fight. Courtney requested permission to make an immediate assault against the enemy positions because he felt that with night falling the advantage of an all-out counterattack lay with the enemy. Permission for the attack was granted, and Courtney briefed his small force and then ordered the advance. Disregarding the danger, he blasted nearby enemy cave positions and machine-gun emplacements. His men, inspired by his leadership and zeal, followed without hesitation. Upon reaching the crest, he waited for more ammunition and reinforcements before continuing. Reinforced by 26 men and an LVT load of grenades, he then drove the remaining enemy off the crest of the hill and ordered his men to dig in. Courtney was killed instantaneously when he led a counterattack to forestall a Japanese Banzai attack. His unwavering devotion to duty in the face of constant enemy fire was truly in the best tradition of the United States Marine Corps.

Meanwhile the 1st Marine Division had been fighting under the guns of the Shuri hills. Here the 1st Division and the 77th Infantry Division encountered the Wana defenses, northwest of Shuri. Behind the Wana Ridge flowed the Asa River and the deep Wana Gorge. The Japanese had fortified Hill 55 overlooking the Gorge and the Marines had to take it. The 5th and 7th Marines moved against it from opposite sides. The 7th Marines, after five days of continuous heavy fighting to take the Ridge, lost 51 killed and 387 wounded in action. On 19 May the 1st Marines relieved them. The 1st Marines then immediately assaulted the ridge with grenades and heavy

Right: Three Japanese
soldiers carry their wounded
friend to safety having decided
to surrender rather than fight
to death.

160

Left: The Japanese used this church as a snipers' nest during the fighting on the Shuri Line.

Left: Rooting out resistance, Marines wait for survivors to emerge from a cave defense which has just been attacked.

Below: Colonel Francis
Fenton prays at the foot of
his son's grave. His son, only
19, had been killed during
the bitter fighting on the
road to Shuri.

Below right: Marines flush
out Japanese from a cane field.

automatic weapons fire and succeeded in taking the crest. By 20 May the 5th Marines had managed to capture the western end of Hill 55 and were moving into the draw. But the Japanese still held 110 Meter Hill, and this made it virtually impossible for the Marines to advance on Shuri. Again the rains came and turned the entire island into a vast sea of mud through which absolutely nothing could move. By 28 May the rains had stopped and the advance began again. Tuesday, 29 May, witnessed the 1st Battalion, 5th Marines taking Shuri Castle. Okinawa was practically secured. So far, Lieutenant General Buckner's Army had sustained 5655 killed and 23,909 wounded in action, while the Japanese had lost over 62,000 dead.

Finally, fresh Marines arrived to bolster up the tired Assault Force; these were Colonel Clarence Walker's 8th Marines, 2nd Division. By the middle of June the Japanese defenses were weakening appreciably. Lieutenant General Buckner decided on 18 May to visit the front to see the 8th Marines go into action. He was witnessing the advance from the 3rd Battalion's observation post when an enemy shell struck nearby and blew a piece of coral into the general's chest. Buckner died soon after.

On that same day Ushijima issued his last order appointing an officer to continue the fight against the US as guerrilla warfare.

Above: A Grumman TBM
torpedo bomber on a mission
over Okinawa. Two Avengers
were responsible for sinking
the *Yamato* on its last mission
to Okinawa.

Left: Lieutenant Colonel
Richard Ross raises the
American flag on the Shuri
Castle.

Above: Acting Marine Mess Sergeant Corporal Nelson Deffner tests his food to reassure the other Marines that the chow is edible.

Japanese soldiers for the first time were surrendering *en masse*. On 19 June 343 surrendered. On 21 June Ushijima prepared for ritual suicide and following a sumptious banquet the Japanese general and his deputy, Cho, died in the early hours of 22 June. Although Buckner's temporary replacement, Major General Roy Geiger, was able to declare that Okinawa was secure on 21 June fighting continued until the end of the month. The final official casualty figures for the 82-day campaign were excessively high: enemy losses were 107,539 counted dead, a further estimate of 23,764 assumed dead in caves or buried by the Japanese, and 10,755 soldiers who gave themselves up. These figures were estimated by the Tenth Army in-

telligence to include 42,000 civilians killed in the fighting by both sides. US losses amounted to 7374 killed, 31,807 wounded and 230 missing. There were also 26,221 non-battle casualties. These figures were a gloomy indication of the scale of casualties which might be incurred once the US invaded Japan.

The Americans had brought the war one step nearer to Japan and were now preparing for the greatest amphibious operation of all time – the invasion of Japan. They had brought the amphibious techniques of landing to new heights as British observers commented 'this operation was the most audacious and complex enterprise which has yet been undertaken by the American Amphibious Forces . . . .'

Above: First Lieutenant David Duncan followed the Marines through the Pacific War and took many photographs for the Marine Corps. He crawled into the belly tank of a P-38 to take a picture.

Left: Duncan explains to an old Okinawan the working of his camera.

A *Fletcher* Class destroyer heads toward Japan during the last months of the war.

9 JAPAN
The Bombing Offensive

Right: Major General Claire
Lee Chennault surrounded by
men of the 14th Air Force.
Until the USAAF had bases
on the Marianas all bombing
raids on Japan were flown by
the 14th AF based in China.

Below: Major General Ira
Eaker and Lieutenant General
Carl Spaatz were both
advocates of strategic
bombing.

Below right: Major General
Curtis Lemay, commander
of the 20th Bomber Group
which flew missions on Japan.

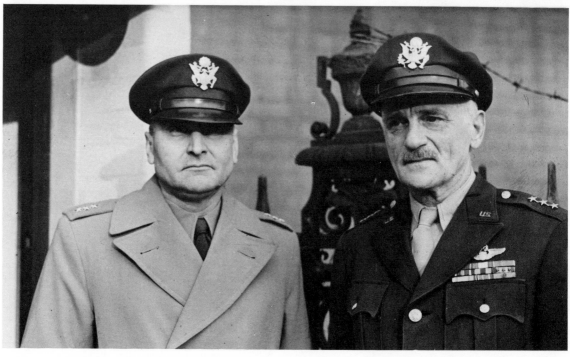

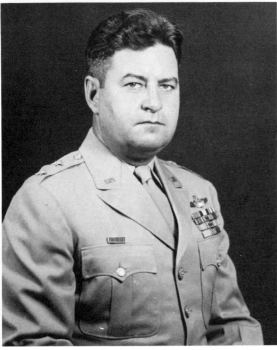

In December 1940 Secretary of the Treasury, Henry Morgenthau, presented a rather strange proposal to President Roosevelt. Despite American neutrality in the Sino-Japanese war, it was suggested that a number of B-17 bombers should be given to the Chinese leader, Chiang Kai-shek, on the understanding that they would be used to attack Tokyo. Roosevelt gave his enthusiastic support, having watched with growing concern the Japanese air raids upon Chinese cities since 1937, and Chiang Kai-shek, understandably, was delighted. Unfortunately on 22 December General George Marshall, Chief of Staff of the US Army, pointed out that there was a shortage of B-17s for his own air service and that none could be spared for the Chinese venture. Reluctantly, the plan was dropped.

Bearing this episode in mind, it might be imagined that the bombing of the Japanese homeland, with the familiar aims of destroying both civilian morale and the industrial base of the country, would have been initiated by the Americans immediately after Pearl Harbor. This was not the case. With the exception of a daring raid upon Tokyo by carrier-launched B-25 twin-engined bombers, led by Colonel James Doolittle on 18 April 1942, no American aircraft assaulted the air space of Japan until June 1944. It was not that Americans did not want to hit the enemy homeland but that, for a wide variety of reasons, they were incapable. The story of the campaign is a classic example of the practical problems confronting even the most sophisticated nation in the organization and conduct of strategic bombing, reinforcing the lessons of both the British and American offensives against Germany. Yet, ironically, the raids against Japan, culminating in those using atomic weapons in August 1945, probably came closer to vindicating the theories of people like Douhet and Mitchell than any others before or since.

Plans for a bombing campaign against Japan bubbled just beneath the surface of American strategy throughout 1942, but foundered on the first and most persistent problem – that of geography. With the massive expansion of her Empire in the aftermath of Pearl Harbor, Japan had created an extensive buffer zone around the home islands, leaving America in possession of no territory from which existing bombers could operate. A continuation of

Doolittle's idea of using carriers was impractical, for even presuming any could be spared, Japanese sea supremacy, particularly in home waters, was so secure that they would be extremely vulnerable. One possibility, suggested by Roosevelt himself, was the stationing of bombers in the eastern provinces of Russia, but Stalin, after lengthy prevarication, refused permission. This left only China – the area originally proposed in 1940 – but the practical problems were immense. To begin with, there was a complete lack of suitable airfields and an apparently insuperable problem of supply, with no Chinese ports open to traffic and the Burma Road cut by advancing Japanese armies. In addition, even if air bases were constructed there was no guarantee that Chiang Kai-shek's troops could protect them for long enough to get a bombing campaign going. Finally – and this was perhaps the overriding problem – there was no aircraft in American service with the range to carry bombs from Central China to Japan – a trip of 1500 miles. Such considerations, coupled with the pressing need to stem the Japanese tide of victory in the Pacific, prevented the planning of a bombing campaign for the first 20 months of the Far Eastern war.

But Roosevelt never gave up the idea entirely. At the Casablanca Conference in January 1943 he discussed the possibility of bombing Japan with the British, and seven months later at Quebec finally decided, in the absence of any other remotely feasible option, to launch the raids from Central China. According to the President's arguments, the problems of supply and ground protection could be solved by basing the bombers in eastern India and merely refueling them at special fields around Changsha on their journeys to and from Japan, while the question of range would be answered as soon as a new bomber, the Boeing B-29 Superfortress, became available. In theory it all sounded very straight-forward, but in practice the problems were only just beginning.

The first of these concerned the B-29 itself. It owed its origins to the American air expansion of 1939, when Roosevelt, worried about events in Europe, had successfully pressed for the formation of a viable strategic bombing arm. Major General Henry Arnold, Chief of the Air Corps, immediately instigated an in-

Top left: Children come running out during an air raid on Tokyo.

Left: A North American P-51, nicknamed *My Girl*, takes off from Iwo Jima. The Mustangs flew as escorts to the B-29s.

Above: The devastation of Tokyo following the night of 9-10 March, when 279 B-29s dropped 190,000 incendiary bombs on the capital. Seventeen square miles were destroyed and 72,000 people died.

quiry into long-term needs, and this concluded that a 'Very Long-Range' bomber was essential. A statement of desired characteristics was drafted and sent to leading aircraft manufacturers in America, asking for designs and contract bids. When these were received in May 1940, two were chosen for prototype construction, although it was apparent that the one from Boeing was potentially the winner. It was a radical design, contemplating an enormous machine with a wing span of 141ft and a fuselage 93ft long. It was expected to enjoy a top speed of 382mph at 25,000ft, a range in excess of 7000 miles and a bomb-carrying capacity of 2000lbs, the whole being protected by ten .50in machine guns and a 20mm cannon in the tail. A wooden mock-up was ready for inspection by November 1940, and the air chiefs were so impressed that six months later, before the aircraft had even been test flown, an order for 250 was put in. Boeing built a completely new factory at Wichita, Kansas, and the first squadrons were confidently expected to be ready for service by late 1943. This deadline was never satisfied as delays in the development of the B-29 followed one upon the other.

The main difficulty arose because throughout the development phase the Boeing engineers were constantly breaking new technological ground. Their most persistent bugbear was weight. An aircraft of this size and potential was necessarily heavy to start with, but as new requirements arose from combat experience over Germany in 1942 and 1943, the addition of self-sealing fuel tanks and armor plating increased the weight considerably. Even after a special 'weight reduction board' had dispensed with such luxuries as soundproofing in the cabin and auxiliary crew bunks, the aircraft was still an incredible 105,000lbs, without the addition of bombs. It clearly required extremely powerful engines just to get off the ground. Four Wright R-3350 18-cylinder, air-cooled power packs were chosen, but they presented an entirely new range of problems. When the first prototype was eventually rolled out for testing in early September 1942 it was found that the engines were barely able to last an hour without burning up and, even after extensive modifications, it was engine failure which, on 18 February 1943, caused the second prototype to

Above: Tokyo's main street, Ginza, in ruins. Only concrete buildings survived the fire raids.

crash, killing the test pilot Eddie Allen and his entire crew of Boeing experts. This alone set the production program back by four or five months. At the same time other new design features were being constantly introduced, the most impressive of which was a novel type of armament system incorporating a small automatic computer which had the capability of correcting the guns for range, altitude, air speed and temperature, as well as a central control mechanism which enabled any gunner (except the man in the tail) to take over more than one of the five power-driven turrets. Such innovations necessitated more electrical power than the existing generators could provide, so 125 new electric motors had to be fitted to each aircraft. All this took time, until by spring 1943 it began to look as if the B-29 was never going to enter squadron service, let alone deliver bombs to Japan.

In an effort to speed the process up, the Army Air Force decided to take over the entire program itself, and on 18 April 1943 Arnold authorized the establishment of a 'B-29 Special Project' under Brigadier General Kenneth Wolfe. He was given responsibility for production, test-flights and crew training and, as commander of the newly-activated 58th Bombardment Wing, directed to prepare the B-29s for commitment to China by the end of the year. This was an impossible schedule, for by December 1943, although Wolfe was well ahead with a scheme to train 452 crews, each of 11 men, the aircraft were still not available. Only 67 of his pilots had even seen a B-29 and preliminary training was being carried out in B-17s. As a result, just before the Cairo Conference of that month, Arnold was forced to report that the bombing of Japan could not begin until mid-1944 – two and a half years after Pearl Harbor. Roosevelt was bitterly disappointed and did not disguise his anger, insisting that the first raid should be carried out no later than 1 May 1944.

But production problems at Boeing were not that easy to solve. By the beginning of 1944 only 97 B-29s had been built, and of these only 16 were flyable. The rest were at special conversion centers, undergoing yet another series of modifications. On 15 January Wolfe – now in control of 20th Bomber Command, of which the 58th Wing was only a part – had no aircraft at all ready for combat, and the new

Presidential deadline looked as unattainable as the old. Once again, Arnold had to intervene, this time to sort out the troubles at the conversion centers. By taking personal charge of the whole process he managed, by force of personality, to get the planes moving at last, and in late March the first battle-worthy B-29 was handed over to Wolfe. By 15 April 150 were ready, being flown to India as soon as crews could be provided. The problems were by no means over – a number of bombers crashed *en route* because of over-heated engines, necessitating further delaying modifications – but by 8 May 148 had arrived in the Far Eastern theater. They were stationed originally at Kharagpur, Chakulia, Pairdoba and Dudhkundi in eastern India, but as early as 24 April a number flew 'over the Hump' of the Himalalayan foothills to the forward bases around Chengtu in Central China. Almost immediately, new problems emerged to delay the start of the offensive still further.

The first of these was supply, for despite a declared intention to make 20th Bomber Command completely self-sufficient, with its own transport element of C-46s, Wolfe soon found that he could not move sufficient stocks of fuel and bombs from India to Chengtu in time for a first raid on 1 May. Even when he stripped B-29s down and used them as transports, he was only able to deliver 1400 tons of supplies to the Chinese bases by that date, and of the 660,000 gallons of fuel needed, he had less than 400,000 on hand. He was forced to call upon the extremely hard-pressed Air Transport Command in the theater, but this brought him into conflict with local commanders, jealous of the official independence of the bombing squadrons. Consequently it was not until early June that a preliminary mission against railway stock at Bangkok could take place and not until 14 June that the first raid upon Japan could be launched. Seventy-five bombers were briefed to attack the iron and steel works at

Midget submarines in the bomb-damaged drydock at Kure. Some 500 submarines were planned for local defense, but only 115 units had been completed by the time of Japan's surrender in August 1945.

Yawata on the island of Kyushu, with depressing results. Seven B-29s aborted before leaving their bases because of mechanical trouble, four returned early for the same reason, three crashed on take off or landing and one came down in China. Of the remainder, 32 were forced to drop their bombs by radar because of cloud cover, 21 failed to locate the target and six jettisoned their loads indiscriminately. Little damage was inflicted.

Nevertheless, Washington was impressed, and on 16 June Wolfe was directed to send his bombers 'the length and breadth of the Japanese Empire.' He was unable to oblige. Fuel stocks in China had been virtually exhausted by just one raid and logistical problems were so bad that it was impossible to build up supplies quickly. The Washington demand was unrealistic, and Wolfe said so. In early July he was recalled to America and replaced by Major General Curtis LeMay, a man of considerable experience, having commanded a B-17 squadron in Europe. He did not arrive until 29 August, and during the intervening period Wolfe's deputy, Brigadier General La

Verne Saunders, continued as best he could. Kyushu was revisited by 15 B-29s on 7 July, fuel stocks were carefully restored, and on 9 and 10 August respectively, long-range attacks were made against steel works at Anshan in Manchuria and fuel plants at Palembang in Sumatra, the latter involving a stop-over at RAF bases in Ceylon. The results, however, continued to be poor and the Japanese began to react, destroying their first four B-29s on 20 August when Yawata was revisited. It was a very slow and unsatisfactory start to what should have been a 'decisive' campaign.

When LeMay arrived, he immediately introduced a series of new tactical ideas based upon his experiences in Europe. He insisted upon adherence to the prevailing B-17 doctrine of high-altitude, precision attacks in daylight, organized the B-29 squadrons into self-defending 'box' formations, and even borrowed the British technique of 'pathfinder' crews to lead the attack and mark a suitable aiming point. These innovations certainly improved the character of the bombing as well as crew morale, but did nothing to solve the basic

Right: A general view of
wrecked aircraft of the
Japanese Air Force at Atsugi
Airport, in September 1945.
The majority of missions
flown in the last months of
the war were kamikaze.

problem of supply. All fuel and bombs had still
to be flown from India to the Chinese bases – a
journey of more than 1000 miles by air which
actually consumed more gasoline than was
being delivered – and this meant the raids upon
Japan were spasmodic, lacking the concentrated force which was needed to make them effective. If long-term damage was to be inflicted,
more convenient bases, situated in good supply
areas and, ideally, closer to Japan, had to be
found. This was realized as early as 1943, before
the Chinese operations had ever begun, when
Admiral Ernest King, US Chief of Naval
Operations, recommended the seizure of the
Mariana Islands 'at the earliest possible date,
with the establishment of heavy bomber bases
as the primary mission.' Full approval was
granted at the Cairo Conference of December
1943, although time was clearly needed before
the process could be fully effected. The
Chengtu-based raids, despite their problems,
had to be continued at least until the Marianas
had been seized and airfields constructed. In
the event, they were not phased out until early
1945 having, in the final analysis, achieved
little beyond the gaining of invaluable
experience.

The island of Saipan in the Marianas group
was invaded on 15 June 1944 and secured by
9 July, with the neighboring islands of Guam
and Tinian coming under American control a
month later. Work on the airfields began as
quickly as possible (in the case of Saipan while
fighting for possession of the island was still
going on) and the first B-29 landed on 12
October, bringing in the commander of the
recently-activated 21st Bomber Command,
(Brigadier General Hansell Jr). By 22 November more than 100 of the bombers had arrived,
enabling a series of 'shake-down' missions to be
flown, chiefly against tactical targets on the
islands of Truk and Iwo Jima. At first, the
results were poor, with inaccurate bombing
and unnecessary losses, but gradually things
improved. By mid-November Hansell decided
that the time was ripe for a raid on Tokyo –
the first since Doolittle's visit two and a half
years before. The attack was scheduled for 17
July, but the weather closed in, imposing a
delay which lasted a week. The Marianas
operations were beginning to bear a worrying
resemblance to those from China.

This impression was reinforced as the new

campaign eventually got under way. On 24 November 111 B-29s were briefed to attack the Nakajima aircraft plant at Musashi, Tokyo. Seventeen returned early with mechanical trouble, only 24 were able to pinpoint the target, six aborted the mission over Japan, dropping their bombs in the sea, one was shot down by interceptor fighters, one ditched in the Pacific on the return flight. The vast majority unloaded their bombs indiscriminately over the Japanese capital and, needless to say, the specified target was hardly touched. Nor was this an isolated incident, for the pattern was repeated in a number of similar raids and losses mounted steadily. By the end of the year it was apparent that drastic changes were required. The prevailing predilection for high altitude, precision attacks in daylight was clearly not producing the desired results: alternative tactics had to be found. As a first step in this direction, Hansell – a keen advocate of the discredited methods – was relieved on 1 January 1945 and replaced by the more experienced LeMay. He too was a believer in precision bombing, having been influenced by the theories of Billy Mitchell during the interwar period, so any new ideas had to be particularly convincing to make him change his mind. Fortunately, the seeds of doubt had been sown during the last few weeks of his command in China.

The key raid in this process of change had taken place on 18 December 1944 against the Chinese city of Hankow on the Yangtze River, captured by the Japanese in 1938 and rapidly built up into an important military center. It was not a strategic target in the theoretical sense, and LeMay initially refused to contemplate it, but after specific orders from America he agreed to co-operate with the local air commander, Major General Claire Chennault, and commit his B-29s in their normal high-altitude role. Chennault opposed these tactics, however, persuading LeMay to send his bombers in comparatively low (18,000 instead of 25,000ft), carrying incendiaries. The raid was an impressive success. Hankow was hit with over 500 tons of fire-producing bombs which gutted the docks, warehouse areas and surrounding sectors of the city. Some of the fires raged uncontrollably for three days.

The lesson was apparent: as Mitchell had pointed out as early as 1924, Far Eastern cities

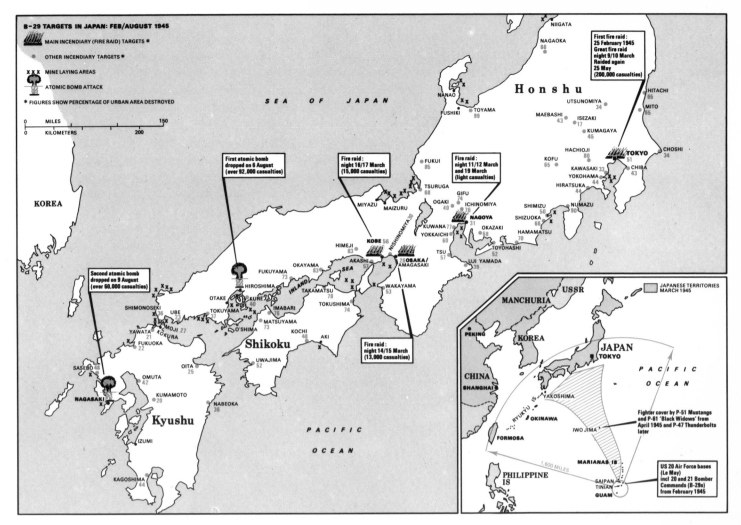

were highly susceptible to fire, being congested and constructed mainly of 'paper and wood or other flammable substitutes.' Precision bombing with high explosives was unnecessary and a waste of effort in such circumstances: area bombing with incendiaries would have a far greater and more immediate effect. The air leaders in America decided to try the switch as soon as news of the Hankow raid came in, issuing orders for test attacks to Hansell on 19 December. Incendiaries, including a newly-developed type containing napalm, which threw out streams of fiercely burning petroleum jelly, were hurriedly shipped out to the Marianas and reports on their use eagerly awaited. But Hansell remained unconvinced – during the time when LeMay was *en route* from China he sent 57 incendiary-carrying B-29s to Nagoya (3 January 1945), but the results were inconclusive – and LeMay himself took some persuading. Only after heavy losses in precision attacks against Tokyo on 27 January did he agree – reluctantly – to switch to fire raids.

The first of the new-style attacks was carried out by 100 B-29s on 4 February against the city of Kobe. Sixty-nine aircraft located the target and results were good: an estimated 2,500,000 square feet of buildings were destroyed or damaged and local industry was clearly disrupted. LeMay was immediately ordered to elevate incendiary raids to top priority and given an extra wing of B-29s to make sure that maximum pressure could be exerted. Gradually, the new bombing philosophy took hold. On 25 February Tokyo was hit and one square mile of buildings destroyed, while on 4 March, on a return visit to the Nakajima plant at Musashi, the old idea of high altitude, precision attack received another blow as 159 B-29s inflicted minimal damage. In fact this particular plant became something of a test case, for after eight separate missions involving a total of 875 aircraft, little more than four percent damage could be discerned. Fire raids were obviously the answer.

Once convinced, LeMay characteristically

Left: Colonel Paul Tibbets poses in front of the *Enola Gay*. Tibbets piloted his B-29 on the mission which dropped the atom bomb on Hiroshima.

devoted his full attention to the new idea, conceiving a major and dramatic change in tactics which involved removing all guns (except the tail) from his B-29s, loading them up with as many incendiaries as they could carry, sending them at night to bomb the target from as low as 5000ft, and guiding them in individually with special pathfinders. Tokyo was chosen as the target and the strike took place on the night of 9/10 March. It was a spectacular success. A total of 279 B-29s, led by pathfinders, arrived over the city between 1200 hours and 0200 hours, high winds fanned the fires that were started and before very long the center of Tokyo was one vast sea of flame. About 16 square miles of buildings were completely leveled and the casualties were enormous. Nearly 84,000 people were killed, 41,000 injured and over a million made homeless, all for the cost of 14 B-29s destroyed.

Thereafter incendiary attacks were made on a sustained level and by the end of the Far Eastern war in August 1945 the statistics of destruction made terrifying reading. At first the major industrial and populous centers of Japan – Tokyo, Nagoya, Kobe, Osaka, Yokohama and Kawasaki – were the primary targets, and by June a total of 105.6 square miles out of an aggregate 257 had been completely destroyed. Within these figures, the damage to individual cities was immense. On the night of 13/14 March 300 B-29s leveled

eight square miles of Osaka, killing 13,135 people; two nights later 15,000 perished in Kobe; on 16 May 170,000 civilians in Nagoya were made homeless as four square miles of the city went up in flames; in two raids against Tokyo on 23 and 25 May, a further 18 square miles were devastated and the city temporarily paralyzed. B-29 losses were by no means light – between March and June well over 100 were destroyed on the fire-raids above – but the results could not be questioned.

Indeed, so impressive were they that by mid-June LeMay was able to report his primary targets destroyed and initiate a secondary campaign against 58 smaller Japanese cities with populations less than 200,000. Beginning on 17 June, when four low-altitude night attacks were launched against Kagoshima, Omuta, Hamamatsu and Yokkaichi, the process soon reached such a stage of sophistication that the B-29s were sent out on such raids every third day until the end of hostilities. This released them to carry out other campaigns against more specific targets such as oil refineries, merchant shipping and airfields, and there were even instances where a return to precision daylight attacks was both possible and effective. The main theme of the offensive remained, however, and the fire raids never lost their top priority rating. By mid-1945 21st Bomber Command appeared to be the most devastating aerial weapon yet devised.

Below: A view of the area of Hiroshima on which the bomb was dropped.

Right: Hiroshima, after the
first bomb was dropped.

Below right: This couple
were killed by the fall out
from the atomic bomb as
they slept.

However the strategy of ending the war through such raids did not succeed. Japanese industry certainly suffered, particularly from a process of dispersion away from city areas, which began as early as 1944, but was still managing to produce essential items right up to the end of the war. The fact that something like 8000 aircraft had been stockpiled in the home islands to be used as a last defensive resort should the Allies invade, shows that not all the factories had been burnt out by mid-1945. Similarly, the Japanese people did not panic and civilian morale remained at an adequate, if rather stoical, level throughout the fire raids. In other words, the lessons of this offensive would appear to be the same as those of the offensive against Germany: that the mounting of a strategic bombing campaign is time consuming, costly and fraught with problems, that the bomber does not always get through to hit precision targets by daylight, necessitating a switch to night-time area bombing to counteract losses and lack of results, and that civilian panic and the destruction of the enemy's war industry do not ensue.

However, this was not the end of the story so far as the offensive against Japan was concerned, for by August 1945 the Americans were able to use an entirely new and devastating weapon – the atomic bomb. Arnold had been told of its potential existence as early as July 1943, when he was directed to modify B-29s as delivery platforms, a process which was completed, in the utmost secrecy, by the end of the year. Tests with dummy bombs were carried out at Muroc, California, in February 1944 and five months later a special combat unit was organized under the command of Colonel Paul Tibbets. Known as the 393rd Bombardment Squadron, it was part of a completely self-sufficient 509th Composite Wing which was to be based, again in secrecy, on the island of Tinian in the Marianas. The first of the modified B-29s left the United States in May 1945 and by July the entire Wing was in place, ready to go. It was just in time. On 16 July the scientists responsible for the Manhattan Project successfully tested the first atomic device in the New Mexican desert, the news was flashed to President Truman at the Potsdam Conference and permission immediately granted to use the weapon against Japan. From what was known of its destructive capability, an atomic

explosion in an enemy city seemed sure to end the war, hopefully without the need for a costly seaborne invasion.

A mission directive was forwarded to Tibbets on 24 July, setting the first – and, it was hoped, the only – strike for 6 August against Hiroshima, with Kokura and Nagasaki as alternative targets in case of bad weather. Problems, for once, were few, however, and at 0245 hours on the specified morning Tibbets took off from Tinian in a B-29 nicknamed *Enola Gay*. He found the primary target in good visibility, dropping his bomb from high altitude at 0915 hours before banking sharply away to escape the blast. Within minutes a tremendous explosion, equivalent to the conventional bomb loads of 2000 B-29s, had killed 78,000

people in Hiroshima and injured a further 51,000. It completely destroyed some 48,000 buildings, damaged another 22,000 and left 176,000 people homeless. The Japanese were stunned, but because of communications problems it took time for the government to react. By 8 August the Imperial Cabinet had still not met and the Americans began to doubt the inevitability of surrender. Truman authorized a second raid, using the only other atomic bomb in existence, and on the morning of 9 August Major Charles Sweeney set out in *Bock's Car*. His primary target was Kokura, but after three abortive bombing runs in poor weather, he switched to his secondary, alternative objective, Nagasaki. At 1100 hours he released his bomb, killing 35,000 and injuring a

further 60,000 of the inhabitants. The Japanese decision to surrender was taken by the Cabinet a few days later, although the clinching factor in the decision was Soviet Russia's declaration of war a few days earlier.

Ignoring the tremendous moral problems involved in the two atomic attacks, the results were exactly what the interwar theorists had always argued. An enemy power had been forced to surrender by air action, without the need for decisive land or naval operations. Up to this point, conventional high explosives or incendiaries had lacked the degree of instantaneous destruction needed to undermine civilian morale or devastate the industrial base, but this was now provided by atomic weapons. The lessons of earlier campaigns therefore tended to be ignored and the new capability emphasized. Regardless of arguments about the inevitability of Japanese surrender because of naval and land victories in the Pacific, the lesson seemed to be that strategic bombing, using atomic bombs, could work. It was a dangerous lesson, particularly when in 1949 the Russians exploded their first atomic device and threatened America with an equal degree of urban destruction should she try to repeat the Japanese attacks against Soviet targets. Japan may have been forced to surrender in 1945, but the weapon used was soon nullified through the process of deterrence, leaving conventional bombs and warfare as the only viable alternative in a situation short of total, self-destructive war.

Below: General MacArthur signs the Japanese instrument of surrender on behalf of the Allies. The ceremony took place on the USS *Missouri* on 2 September 1945 in Tokyo Bay. Behind MacArthur are Generals Wainwright (left) and Percival, who had spent the war in prisoner of war camps.

Marines stand at attention as the Japanese Mission prepares to leave the USS *Missouri* after the surrender ceremony was over.

INDEX

PICTURE CREDITS

Bison Picture Library
14/15, 26 (top), 47 (center), 50/51, 71 (top), 80, 85 (left), 98/99, 104 (bottom), 113 (center), 144 (top), 168 (bottom), 176, 177, 184 (inset), 187

Imperial War Museum
56 (center 2), 105 (bottom), 110 (bottom)

Mainichi Newspapers
170 (inset), 172/173

National Archives
9, 16/17, 20 (bottom), 23 (top), 25 (center), 34 (top), 36/37 (all 3), 39 (both), 42 (top), 43, 44/45, 47 (top), 48/49 (both), 52, 54 (both), 56 (top), 60/61, 64 (top), 65, 67 (all 3), 69 (center), 71 (bottom 2), 73, 82/83, 85 (right), 86 (top), 87, 90, 91, 92, 95, 100

(bottom), 102/103, 104 (top), 106 (inset), 111 (bottom), 113 (top), 114 (top), 141 (bottom), 144 (bottom), 148 (top), 161 (bottom), 166/167, 169 (bottom), 186

National Maritime Museum
144 (center)

Robert Hunt Library
173

United States Air Force
18/19, 88/89 (both), 93, 124, 125, 168/169 (top), 170/171, 174/175, 178/179, 180, 182/183

United States Army
101 (bottom), 184/185

United States Marine Corps
62/63, 69 (top and bottom), 72 (both), 74/75, 76/77, 78/79, 96/97 (both), 120/121, 122/123, 128/129, 134/135, 136, 137 (all 3), 138, 140 (all 4), 141 (top 2), 145 (bottom), 148 (bottom), 149 (all 3), 152 (both), 157 (bottom), 160 (both), 161 (top), 162 (both), 163 (both), 164, 165 (both), 188/189

United States Navy
6/7, 8, 10/11, 12 (both), 20 (top), 24, 25 (top and bottom), 26 (bottom), 27, 29, 30/31, 32/33, 35 (all 3), 42 (bottom), 46 (both), 47 (bottom), 55, 56 (bottom), 58, 64 (bottom), 81, 84 (both), 86 (bottom), 94, 100 (top), 101 (top), 106/107, 117, 126/127, 130/131, 132, 133, 139, 142/143, 145 (top), 146, 147, 153 (both), 154 (both), 155 (both), 157 (top), 158 (both), 159